All Her Children

Books by *Dan Wakefield*

Island in the City: *The World of Spanish Harlem*
Revolt in the South
The Addict: *An Anthology*
Between the Lines
Supernation at Peace and War
Going All the Way
Starting Over
All Her Children

All Her Children

Dan Wakefield

DOUBLEDAY & COMPANY
GARDEN CITY, NEW YORK
1976

PHOTO CREDITS

American Broadcasting Companies, Inc.—Photographs No. 2, 3, 4, 5, 6, 8, 10
Ed Eckstein—No. 1
Howard C. Gray—No. 7
Doris A. Weston—No. 9
Bill Powers—No. 11

Library of Congress Cataloging in Publication Data

Wakefield, Dan.
    All her children.

    1. All my children. I. Title.
PN1992.77.A5W3   791.45'7
ISBN 0-385-11086-3
Library of Congress Catalog Card Number: 75-14845

To Eva M. DeRosset,
with whom I am home

We are all like Scheherazade's husband,
in that we want to know what happens next.
    —E. M. Forster

I have been fortunate to escape what has
been called "that form of snobbery which can
accept the Literature of Entertainment in the
Past, but only the Literature of Enlightenment
in the Present."
    —Raymond Chandler

CONTENTS

CONTENTS

HOW I GOT
HOOKED

I was a closet soap opera addict.

I state the fact baldly because I have hidden it for so long now, and in declaring my addiction in public I hope to encourage others to rid themselves of the shame and guilt that have tormented them, to lift up their chins and say to their loved ones, their colleagues, their peers: I like to watch daytime television serials even though I am not necessarily a housewife, a maid, or an account executive for a leading detergent. I am, irrespective of age, sex, or profession, a devoted fan of one or more of the Monday-through-Friday programs that are most commonly and disparagingly known as soap operas.

It has always been socially acceptable for housewives to watch soap opera, but the popular image of the sort of housewife who would actually watch them is a gross composite of the cartoon "Hazel the Maid" and Shirley Booth playing the slatternly heroine of *Come Back, Little Sheba*. No self-respecting wife and mother with an education and a membership in the League of Women Voters or a tattered copy of *The Catcher in the Rye* left over from her first literary awakening as an adolescent would easily admit to being a soap opera fan. As for a man who would watch a daytime TV serial—*well*. You can imagine why I found it difficult to explain, and kept it secret. But that is the coward's way out, and I want to make a clean breast of it once and for all.

As we all know only too well by now, the origins of socially aberrant behavior can be found in childhood, and my own case is no exception. I grew up in the heart of the Midwest in the 1930s and 1940s (b. 1932), and hurried home from grade school to listen to the radio soap operas, the daily stories of "Our Gal Sunday," "The Romance of Helen Trent," "Stella Dallas," and "Just Plain Bill, Barber of Hartville." Sometimes on beautiful sunny afternoons, as I sat indoors with my ears glued to the radio, my mother would ask with concern if I didn't want to go outside and play. I averted my eyes and mumbled maybe I'd do that later, after I'd listened to "Young Widder Brown." For an apparently healthy American boy to sit indoors and listen to "Young Widder Brown," when he could have been out playing baseball or frolicking with his faithful dog Spot or building a treehouse, was almost as bad as being caught masturbating in the bathroom. Worse still, at least two or three days a week I feigned an upset stomach in order to stay home and lie around listening to the soap operas that were on during school hours.

Despite this neurotic behavior I lived up to most of my responsibilities as a budding good citizen, as witnessed by the honor of being named a member of the Traffic Squad of School #80 when I was twelve years old. This distinction brought with it a white, cross-chest belt of a style reminiscent of the Bengal Lancers and a bright silver badge that looked like a combination police medallion and shield of a Holy Crusader. Accompanying all that glory was the responsibility of being posted on crucial intersections to make sure the little kids watched out for traffic and were sheperded safely across the street on their way to and from school against the dangers of potential cars that occasionally idled by. If the dangers were minimal the trust was sacred, and it is not until now, some thirty years later, that I have publicly admitted that on lunch hours I habitually left my traffic post early in order to hurry home in time to hear the continuing drama of "Ma Perkins," one of the oldest of the radio soap operas. Thank God no straggling toddlers were injured when crossing, unprotected, the sleepy corner of Sixty-third Street and Winthrop Avenue in Indianapolis while I, full of guilt and fascination, sat in the family kitchen devouring, with a peanut butter and jelly sandwich, the trials of kindly old Ma Perkins, her relatives and friends.

As far as I knew at the time, none of my school chums were subject to such illicit cravings. I certainly never mentioned "Ma Perkins" in class, or on the playground; I never discussed it with Richard Turmail, captain of the Traffic Squad, or Eugene Sams, our star elementary school basketball center, or even Dicky Warne, my best friend and the smartest kid in the class. It would have seemed even more humiliating to mention my radio soap opera addiction to, for instance, Carol Rivers, the slim twelve-year-old beauty I had a mad crush on, or Marilyn Hull, who had been my across-the-street neighbor since we both began the first grade.

For several years then I thought I was, as the saying went, "the only kid on the block," which meant in effect the only boy in the sane and civilized world, who listened to such stuff. Then a funny thing happened. In the sophomore year of high school, at some party or other, on somebody or other's front porch or in the backseat of somebody's car at a drive-in, some guy or girl my own age started talking about "Ma Perkins." And instead of the words being greeted by an embarrassed silence, there was a rush of giggling. People started talking of different characters on the program, and imitating their lines and voices, like "Well, if it t'ain't old Shuffle Shofer, just come over from movin' some two-by-fours over to the lumberyard." And then someone else would imitate Ma Perkins in a time of crisis, when she always looked up at the picture of her deceased husband hung above the mantel, and, in an organ-music-backed soliloquy, called upon the shade of "Pa" Perkins, who of course would have known the right thing to do on that or any other occasion, and Ma asked that his spirit give her wisdom or at least strength.

Once Ma Perkins had been admitted, the floodgates of happy confession broke. Both boys and girls (as we were called and called ourselves in those days) came forth with their recollections of Stella Dallas, Helen Trent, and all the rest. I remember trying to impress a bunch of other high school kids by reciting from memory (as I am about to even now) the opening theme of the story stated at the beginning of every episode of "Our Gal Sunday," in which the announcer, in stentorian tones, told us—and we never tired of hearing it—"This is the story that asks the question, Can a girl from a little mining town in Colorado find happiness with the rich and titled Lord Henry Brinthrop of Blackswan Hall?"

To my mixed delight and chagrin, before I was halfway through I was joined by a chorus of voices, reciting the words along with me like a litany.

High school was full of those astounding surprises when you learned that you had not been, after all, "the only one on the block . . ." Even Bill Bosson and Fuzzy Stout, athletes and all-round guys, even Janet Brucker and Mary Ann Hall, popular and pretty girls, all had listened to radio soap operas!

Of course our kidding about those old radio programs was a kind of forties high school version of Camp, sure; and yet I think it was more than that. After all, we *remembered* entire plots and exchanges of dialogue, characters, and events; and if we recalled them with laughter and mockery (to protect ourselves from having taken something too seriously that we feared was not all that sophisticated) those memories were also mixed with fascination and affection.

Ever since the cavemen sat around the fire and recounted and embroidered the tales of their fears and adventures, humans have wanted and needed stories, in whatever form they could get them, all the way from talk to minstrelcy to novels to movies and radio and television. For middle-class Americans of the radio era, those soap operas were our *stories*. Not the only ones, of course, but among the most important ones for many of us, along with the fantasy-style stories of the comic books. As kids then in school we mostly read collections and anthologies, excerpts from *Ivanhoe* and *Hiawatha* and snippets and scraps of other remote material by and about what we delicately referred to as "dead guys."

But the soap opera stories were by and about the kind of people living when we were, people like we knew or might possibly know. They served perhaps an even greater story need for our mothers, most of whom then were stuck at home all day. This was before the paperback revolution, before the boom of book clubs, and even though magazines flourished then, you didn't have to put everything else aside and sit down and read to get the soap opera story; it was told to you while you did the dishes or the ironing. Kids could also be busy with other things, blocks or toys or drawing or coloring pictures and still hear the soap opera stories.

The soap opera got its name of course because the sponsors of the programs were mostly manufacturers of different brands of soap that they hoped to sell to the audience of mostly housewives who listened to the program; and, ironically, "soap" had another connotation of sudsy, fluffy, and insubstantial, characterizing the kind of "operas" these were supposed to be, operas whose only score was the melodramatic organ music swelling and subsiding in the background, while the "operatic" nature of the plot was in its high-pitched overdramatization. A dictionary definition of the radio era said that soap operas were characterized by "little action and much sentiment." They were thought to be sentimental to a fault, supposedly to please the feminine nature, which no one questioned then was basically "sentimental," meaning inclined to quick tears, to sudsy, fluffy emotions.

To say something is "soap opera" means it is not realistic but overdone, overstated, a souped-up story that couldn't really happen to anyone. And yet, and yet . . . no one has ever denied that soap opera is at least an imitation of real life, if an exaggerated one, and there were often times when in some tricky way life seemed to be imitating soap opera, the way for instance it seemed to the late popular journalist and novelist Robert Ruark when he wrote in his syndicated column in the waning era of the radio soap programs that "the average man and woman in this country live a soap opera existence. They travel from crisis to crisis, with bills unpaid, with emergencies, with hopeless troubles."

Everyone, even its followers, kidded soap opera for its built-in formula of continual crisis—but otherwise how could the program keep going, keep holding the listeners' interest? As a boy I think I made my first discovery of storytelling technique when after some years of listening to "Our Gal Sunday" I realized that whenever some great and seemingly insurmountable problem was finally solved, when the skein of a particular plot had run itself out and been resolved, there was always a part in one program when the characters, tired but thankful, simply sat around sipping tea, and discussing matters like the pleasantness of the weather, the rewards of virtue, the felicities of friendship. All was quiet and peaceful; you could hear the reassuring tinkle of the teacups and spoons. "More sugar, Lord Henry?" "Ahh, yes, thank you, dear Sunday. And just a touch of that fresh, rich cream. . . ." After a few minutes of this, while the listeners were still enjoying the deserved respite of the characters from all their trials and had not yet had a chance to grow restless or bored with the uncommon tranquillity, a knock would come at the door. A dire voice would announce: "Telegram for Lord Henry." Even as a small child, I knew that telegram was not a message informing Lord Henry that he had just won the Nobel Peace Prize, or even taken first place in the local Garden Show. Oh no. That telegram, friends and neighbors, could only be bad news, the beginning of another set of trials and tribulations. These little interim scenes were a standard part of the radio serial formula, what we might call the "Tea before the Telegram" syndrome.

This technique or stylistic device of storytelling is also of course a comment on life and fate and all the old themes of man's brief and troubled passage through what the Old Testament (which, with its plagues and miracles and fears and retributions, may be the stern father of all soap opera) calls "this vale of tears." This same sort of device of the short peace between the clamors of life is repeated in some of the most exalted and culturally approved dramas, from Shakespeare to

Ingmar Bergman. The "Tea before the Telegram" reminds me of the "Strawberries and Cream" interlude in Bergman's *The Seventh Seal,* in which the harried characters, having passed through a dangerous storm, enjoy a brief interlude of sunlight and lute music as they share fresh strawberries and cream on the side of a green hill, before, as they finish the last sips and morsels, the specter of Death appears. . . . Most all our stories, whatever their medium, seem to tell us that in the midst of our travails there are brief but lovely moments when we can sit down, breathe easily, and have a little refreshment before the next telegram arrives.

I think the excesses of soap opera, especially in reference to the current, more sophisticated half-hour TV serials, have perhaps been overstressed, been made the butt of condescending criticism of any and all soap opera as a kind of bad impossible dream. When I was trying to describe the current hit soap opera "All My Children" to a very bright woman who couldn't understand why such a program would interest me, she asked if there were any times on the program when there wasn't a crisis, was there any time for instance when characters who were newly married were happy and in love, or was there always an immediate tragedy or crisis to embroil them? I said, "No, for a while everything will be O.K. and they will be happy in their marriage, and some of the other people around them, friends or relatives, will have a big problem and then, maybe after that is solved, the newly married couple, though still in love, may begin to find that all is not rosy, may begin to find conflicts between themselves that might ruin everything. . . ."

My lady friend smiled, with a look that indicated both approval and understanding.

"Oh," she said. "You mean it's like real life!"

"That's it," I said. "Now you're getting it."

I was a latecomer to television soap operas, primarily because I was a latecomer to television of any kind. I am of the last generation in America that grew up without the tube, and to whom its appearance in the lives and homes of friends and acquaintances was a real curiosity. Look! There are pictures of people moving around who are talking and doing things just like in a movie, but it's happening on a little screen in an ordinary person's living room! That is the reaction I had when I saw TV sets operating in the late forties and early fifties. As best I remember, the first time I watched a television program was in my junior year in high school, in 1947, in the living room of Wardie Walker's house. A bunch of us had gathered there to witness this amazing phenomenon, and we giggled and joked and hooted at the program to hide our awe and nervousness. It was a novelty and a luxury rather than an accepted part of daily life, though it seems only a moment in time that the presence of a TV set in the home changed from being regarded as something like owning your own thoroughbred racehorse to something like having your own alarm clock or frying pan or, yes, your own radio—just another standard necessity of life.

When I went to college at Columbia in the early fifties no student would have been caught dead owning his own television set. We were *intellectuals,* you see, and at that time all self-respecting intellectuals feared that television would fry the minds of the masses, make free men into Orwellian robots, and in general turn all of Western culture into a vast wasteland. If there was any bugaboo more feared by intellectuals of the fifties than the hydrogen bomb, it was the television set.

The only television program my friends and I watched in college was the Army vs. McCarthy hearings, a daytime "show" —it was respectable to watch because it was *news* and *history*—though perhaps part of our fascination in seeing it, part of our zeal in cutting classes and going to a neighborhood bar on Broadway to watch the televised proceedings, was that in many ways this was a real-live soap opera! Here was a daily drama starring shady-faced, ominous-voiced Senator Joe McCarthy, who represented for us liberal Columbia students the embodiment of the forces of political evil, and his brightly shining opponent, the craggy-faced, white-haired, crafty-but-kindly old New England lawyer, Joseph N. Welch! There were crises, threats, challenges, and even tears as careers and policies hung in the balance! Tune in tomorrow and see whether good will triumph over evil! For pure soap opera, all it lacked was organ music.

Though it is understandably impossible for people who grew up with television as a fact of life to conceive of this, the anti-intellectual stigma of television persisted with many of my own generation right into adult life. I remember as recently as the early sixties friends in New York City apologizing for buying a TV set, assuring us puritans that they only were going to watch "the good things," which meant news programs and documentaries of condor stalking in the Andes and educational specials with titles like "The World of the Atom." And, well, maybe it wouldn't hurt now and then to watch a ball game or some of the old movies shown late at night—you know, the really *good* old movies, the certified classics, things like *Citizen Kane* and *All Quiet on the Western Front*.

I didn't own a TV set myself until 1961, when I had to buy one as part of a package deal of purchasing furniture in order to get the coveted lease on a good New York apartment with a reasonable rent. Scoff as I did at that boxy old TV set, it soon became a necessity of life, if only for watching ball games and really good old movies of course. I have owned a set ever since.

But would I have watched a soap opera on television back then? How dare it be suggested. As a free-lance writer I worked at home, and could have flipped the switch anytime, but it never occurred to me to watch television when it was light outside (except for a weekend ball game) any more than it would have to mix a batch of martinis for breakfast (in fact, the latter vice was much more likely and socially acceptable). Besides, everyone knew that there was "nothing on" television in the daytime, nothing anyway that anyone with intelligence would deign to watch.

Perhaps like many other people, I started watching daytime television in a time of crisis. It was the holiday season of 1965, and while I consider any holiday season a time of crisis, this one was especially a downer because it was the first one after I had been divorced. It is my private theory that the holiday season—what my friend the free-lance philosopher Art "the Rug" Bernstein labeled "the Trinity" of Thanksgiving, Christmas, and New Year's—is one of the principal means that our society employs to punish those people who do not conform to its rules and standards. It is during the holiday season that we are barraged with the message that any of us who are not part of a family are misfits, kooks, and creeps. We are told in song and story, in advertisements and hymns and posters, in commercials and fund appeals and department-store windows, and by street-corner Santas and Salvation Army brass ensembles, that all men and women of goodwill are members of warm, family units who are gaily and busily stringing their evergreens with popcorn and cranberries, wrapping gifts, roasting turkeys, hanging up stockings, and gathering round the hearth in a continual series of animated Norman Rockwell poses.

The first warning messages of the coming holiday season arrive as early as October, the opening salvos in what will become the psychic saturation bombing of the "holiday spirit." The first message last year was a TV commercial for a stereo record of Christmas music, in which a middle-aged actress stood by a Christmas tree and said how all of us would want to have this record because soon everyone would be gathering with their families to celebrate this time of togetherness. There was no mention or suggestion (there never is) that there might be millions of people out there who are widowed, divorced, estranged from their mates or families, or simply living alone without a lover and far from loved ones in spirit as well as physical distance, and are understandably, humanly, lonely.

I think that if for nothing else I will always love daytime television soap operas for being the only medium that sent me a different message during that dreary post-divorce holiday season. On Christmas Eve day that year I watched one soap opera after another, and was relieved to find the lives of perfectly nice people portrayed who were not all rosy-cheeked with fa-la-la-de-da, but who had troubles, confusions, and traumas whose pain and intensity were heightened by the pressure of the holidays.

On one show, a secretary having an affair with her boss sat alone at a bar while he hurried off to be with his wife and children because it was Christmas Eve. A tear came down the secretary's cheek as she sipped her martini and listened to the jukebox play "White Christmas." On another show, a troubled young college student who was dreading the "vacation" with his parents because of his conflicts with them braced himself for the holiday trip back home by getting a shot of heroin. All of the soaps showed some people in desperation whose plight was made worse by the holiday season.

I don't think troubled viewers dreading their own Christmas season rushed out to get a fix any more than I did, but I would bet that a great many of them shared my relief in seeing that they weren't the only ones having a rough time of it during the season to be jolly.

As an innocent intellectual, I had no idea that the masses out there in videoland were watching everyday stories that dealt with drugs, divorce, abortion, mental illness, loneliness, despair, and other such subjects that were mostly taboo in prime-time viewing. The TV soap operas were different in more than their visual presence from the radio serials of my childhood that they emerged from. Ma Perkins would have surely suffered a coronary on hearing the problems of her television heirs.

Despite my interest and appreciation for television soap operas, I pulled myself back from getting too involved in them. But although I resisted the soaps at home, I took to turning them on while traveling on journalistic assignments, as a respite from interviewing strangers when I returned to my hotel room. I do not pretend that I tuned in the soaps for any professional reasons; it was purely entertainment and relief, yet I began to get from these programs a reverberation of attitudes and moods that I was finding outside among the people and politicians I was talking with about some aspect or other of the state of the nation. While writing a piece for the *Satur-*

day Review on the feelings of people in a town in New Hampshire in response to the Nixon-McGovern campaign, I incorporated something I saw on a soap opera as part of my story. I had interviewed a number of assorted citizens that day who were expressing disillusionment over the first sour smells emanating from Watergate, and I described in my article how:

"Later that afternoon I return to the room and tune in a soap opera in which one of the characters has just resigned from running for governor of his state because he is a pawn of 'The Syndicate' and he can't in good conscience continue following its orders and be its secret puppet candidate. His girl friend is scornful, says she knew of his mob connections all along, and thinks he is crazy to give up his chance to be governor. 'You mean after twenty years you're going moral on me?' she asks with contempt."

Outside in the streets, in bars and cafés, I had been hearing people express their disbelief in politics, their feeling that morality was a public stance to cover private corruption, that "everybody's doing it." And then on the soap, there was the same kind of cynicism, only expressed in dramatic form. In less specific but more pervasive ways I was getting from the TV soap operas a more accurate feel of American society, in tones of thought and talk and dress, than I could find in most newspapers and magazines, and certainly more so than on any of the laugh-tracked, sickly sweet family fantasy-dramas of nighttime "adult" viewing.

By then I had become a real follower of one particular program, the daytime serial "All My Children." The small true touches, the accurate rendering of contemporary styles and feelings, was one of the things that fascinated me about the program. But I can't pretend I got hooked on it because of some sociological interest.

In the spring of 1971 I was living in Los Angeles and recuperating from writing a novel. I choose the word "recuperating" advisedly, believing, as George Orwell said, that writ-

ing a book is like "having a bout with a long illness," and, as
after any long illness, one requires a recovery period, even if
it is just an unconscious kind of living in low gear, idling
around in a sort of disoriented, ambulatory convalescence.

During this period I was greatly cheered by meeting a talented young woman, an artist of considerable brilliance, ambition, and nervousness—as what real artist is not? While she
worked away in her studio she kept a battered television set
going all the time, tuned down low, mostly I think to soothe
her nerves, to have faces and voices to keep her company as
she worked. She could and did tune it in and out of her consciousness, occasionally stopping to face the screen and make a
critical comment, as if she were addressing the people on the
program or the people behind the production of it. On Southern California television some of the most bizarre and entertaining fare is found in the automobile commercials, and at
that time a new car magnate was on the rise, a fellow named
Cal Worthington, who, in a surrealistic attempt to show his
prowess in selling cars, dressed up in cowboy clothes and
wrestled live animals, leopards and tigers and such, in front of
endless rows of his automobiles, while in the background a
singsong chorus did a jingly commercial song with the frantic
refrain—"Go see Cal, go see Cal, go see Cal!" One day during
one of those performances, my artist friend put her hands on
her hips, tilted her head to one side, and uttered one of her
pronouncements (she often spoke in pronouncements).

"You know," she said forcefully, "I don't *trust* that Cal
Worthington!"

Except for such occasional critiques, my artist friend didn't
pay much attention to the continuous programs playing on
her television, with the single and unique exception of the
soap opera "All My Children." Every day when this program
came on she put aside her paints, and I or anyone else present
had to put away books or magazines or anything else that
might be distracting and give full attention to the show.
When she told me I had to watch this soap opera, I asked—
since I didn't know her very well yet—*why?*

"Because," she said, in one of her most official pronouncements, "It's *wonderful.*"

And, as happened so surprisingly often, she was right.

The first time I watched the program with her, she filled me in on the background. As it turned out, she embroidered a bit, but her added touches seem to me now completely faithful to the spirit of the actual story.

One of her ingenious elaborations concerned *Nick Davis,* a principal character who, at the time we were watching, operated a dance studio in Pine Valley, the town where the story takes place. He was also trying to marry *Anne Tyler,* the daughter of one of the town's leading families. Naturally, the leading family of Pine Valley does not want their daughter to marry a guy named *Nick Davis* who runs the local dance instruction studio. My friend told me that *Anne's* family had attempted to buy off *Nick Davis* with the following deal: if he agreed to leave *Anne* alone and not try to marry her, they would buy him the Arthur Murray franchise in Santa Barbara!

I later learned that it's not allowed for the program to mention names of specific products or businesses. My artist friend had added the touch of the Arthur Murray franchise but her instinct was absolutely right, and it would have fit the situation perfectly.

What I first remember about the program is *Nick Davis* coming into view in one of his natty outfits, and my friend pointing to the screen and saying delightedly—"There's *Nick Davis.* You just watch—he's a real *cad!*"

That was the perfect term. *Nick Davis* was not, as he was sometimes unfairly thought to be, a "villain." He was, more precisely, "a real cad."

And, in the ensuing years, I have watched *Nick* mature from his experiences in such a way that he is sometimes a really nice guy, and occasionally he is even victimized a little by other people in Pine Valley. He can no longer even be easily categorized as a plain, ordinary cad. We are seeing that he has his good points, too. We are seeing him change and develop, just like a real person does.

And that's a lot more interesting.

So are all the people in Pine Valley more interesting than they first appear on the surface, the first times you see them. Naturally, it takes a little while of watching the program to figure this out.

If you watch every day, it takes about a week.

Then you're hooked.

In the next few years I watched the program when time and place would permit. I watched my artist friend's thrift-shop black-and-white set that bounced across the floor during the great Southern California earthquake but still could be banged and cajoled into focus most of the time, and a huge color console model in the living room of a farmhouse in West Branch, Iowa. I watched sets in hotel and motel rooms across the country, and back in Boston when I settled into a townhouse, it was first furnished with what had become the bare necessities of my life: a desk, a bed, and a television set.

What with all the moving around and assorted professional and personal interruptions, I sometimes missed the program for as much as a month at a time, but one of the beauties is that when you tune back in, within two or three days you are in the swing of things and up on most of the doings in Pine Valley.

I was moved when the straight, pure-of-heart young *Tara Martin* secretly married *Phil Brent* (without benefit of clergy) when he was drafted and sent to Vietnam; I bit my nails in worry when *Phil* was reported missing in action and *Tara*, pregnant with his child, married *Phil's* best friend, *Chuck Tyler*. I wondered if such a marriage could work, especially after *Phil* was found by Vietnamese peasants who slowly nursed him back to health and an inevitable return to Pine Valley. I gnashed my teeth as the cad *Nick Davis* insidiously undermined the marriage of *Anne Tyler* and the upstanding lawyer *Paul Martin,* shook my head as the beautiful and neu-rotic *Erica Kane* complained and nagged and wore down the spirit of her husband, the handsome and sincere young *Dr. Jeff Martin,* and I was of course relieved when after they split

Dr. Jeff met the modest and admiring young new nurse at the Pine Valley Hospital, *Mary Kennicott*, and they fell deeply in love. If only the jealous *Erica* didn't ruin things for them, I knew they had a chance to find happiness together. . . .

Following the program was fun, and beyond the pure entertainment I began to be fascinated with what must lie behind it—the professional skill and imagination involved in turning out a continuous story five days a week, fifty-two weeks a year, with a cast of several dozen characters interacting with one another in daily situations dramatic enough and believable enough to hold the interest of a mass nationwide audience, without the lures of cops, crime, eroticism, or violence.

It occurred to me that the daytime TV serials are one of the major forms of storytelling for a whole segment of our society, and yet they are largely neglected in any serious discussion of contemporary entertainment. The categorical term "soap opera" is simply used to dismiss such programs altogether, as if by their name and its definition they are by nature of no value or consequence. I was amazed to find that in most books written on American television, soap operas are not mentioned at all. In going through the indexes of a dozen or so such books published in the last five years, I could not even find soap opera or serials listed. Under "S" I found a number of fascinating subjects, including Saudi Arabia, Gilbert Seldes, sex differences in viewing habits, and Pierre Salinger. As for the daytime serials watched by nearly forty million people each week—no soap.

There is not even a mention of soap opera in a book called *TV: The Business Behind the Box,* published in 1971, though by then daytime programming—which is divided between soap operas and game shows—accounted, as it does today, for an estimated 75 per cent of the revenue of the major networks. When I began talking with people who work in the production of daytime serials, almost every one of them mentioned that figure, and as one noted ruefully, "we support the prime-time stuff, we support the fancy and expensive and elaborate programs that get all the hoopla and reviews and acclaim, and yet it's as if we don't even exist."

I finally found three useful books devoted to the subject of radio and television soap opera in America—*The Soaps*, by Madeline Edmondson and David Rounds; *The Serials*, by Raymond W. Stedman; and *The Wonderful World of TV Soap Opera*, by Bob LaGuardia. All these books are, in their own ways, of interest and value to the fans or students of this phenomenon as it was born and has grown in this country.

Until I started doing even the most cursory investigation of the soap opera field I did not know that there is a growing subculture, what might be called a "soap opera underground," in America, complete with a variety of fan magazines such as *Afternoon TV* and *Daytime TV Stars*, that tells of the private lives of the soap players, news of the programs, and reports of fan-club activities in the style of the old movie fan mags. And, for fans fearful of missing any part of the plot of their favorite soaps, there is now a monthly newsletter with subscribers all across the country and abroad that summarizes the stories of all the daytime serials.

I did not know that it wasn't until 1973 that the television industry made its first token recognition of soap operas as a valid part of dramatic programming by awarding a "special" Emmy to the outstanding actress of daytime serials. I was of course delighted to learn that the award went to Mary Fickett, who plays the role of nurse *Ruth Martin* on "All My Children." (In 1975 the industry televised a special Emmy awards show for all daytime programming.)

If all this stirred my interest as a journalist and helped justify my desire to write about my own favorite soap opera, I still knew, deep down, that I wanted to write about "All My Children" for what I consider the best reason of all: I had grown to love it. When I wrote to Agnes Nixon, the "creator" and head writer of the program, asking to see her and have her co-operation in writing about the show, I said, in all honesty, "I come as a fan."

When I wrote that letter in August 1974 I had no idea that, only a few weeks before, "All My Children" had, after not quite five years on the air, risen to the top of the television daytime serial ratings. I was pleased to find that far from being what I had come to consider a private passion of my own, "All My Children" was the object of a growing cult of avid fans across the country, not only in kitchens but on college campuses, where it is religiously watched by loungefuls of students, and that as well as being a new collegiate entertainment craze it has also become a part of the curriculum in a number of universities where it is being taught in courses on contemporary American civilization.

The "All My Children" phenomenon is part of a confluence of different forces that are making soap opera respectable. Part of the soap stigma has been washed off by the tremendous popularity of the English serial "Upstairs, Downstairs," in which the underlying theme of reviews and discussions invariably include debate on whether it is "really just a soap opera." I am sure that the fact it is English in origin has helped break down our native snobbery toward the serial form in general. And in fact that is what soap opera really is— the same basic concept of serial drama that is as old as storytelling, as old as *The Arabian Nights* and "once upon a time" and "in our next episode we shall learn what happens to . . ." It is the old form of serial storytelling practiced pre-electronics by Dickens and Dostoevsky and Henry James as they shaped their novels in installments to be read in sequential issues of periodicals.

I am not about to stake a theoretical claim that soap is the latest "art form of the future," destined to bury the novel, the feature film, the stage, the nighttime TV detective programs, the street theater, and Andy Warhol-inspired happenings, or in fact any other form of dramatic entertainment. But I do believe the television soap opera is a valid and important and, God knows, popular part of the spectrum of contemporary entertainment, and is worthy of discussion and appreciation as such, with all its built-in restrictions of time and production. The originality and excellence of "All My Children" make it not only a marvelous kind of entertainment, but also, like all good storytelling, a reflection of the way we live now, and the way we wish we lived.

The almost sudden discovery of "All My Children" by academics and collegians and reporters has both pleased and bemused the people who work on the show. When Agnes Nixon told me an Ohio State professor had written her to say he wanted to assign the program in his anthropology course, Agnes speculated, in her usual style, whether the course would be called "Coming of Age in Pine Valley."

Maybe it is not only Pine Valley but the locales of all the fourteen daytime TV serials that at last have begun to come of age in the consciousness of the country. They have been a major part of our society's imaginative landscape for some time, but their existence has now begun to be acknowledged in the eyes of many people who for so long pretended that they weren't there at all, or if they were, that they didn't count. The shock of recognition has for many of us been a delight and has kept us watching and tuning in tomorrow and tomorrow as I now do—and wondering, as I did, how it all happened, how it's done, who does it and where and how and why—which is what this book is about, mainly through the focus of my own favorite program.

I have named the parts of the book with the equivalent terms that are used in a script for a daytime television serial— beginning with a "Prologue," followed by a series of five "Acts," and ending with a "Beauty Shot," which is a view, without dialogue, of some place or a person or persons who were important in that day's story. The usual script has four Acts and six commercial breaks. This book will have five Acts, but no commercial interruptions.

The reader should understand that my interviews with the people who write, produce, and act in "All My Children" and my visits to the studio and sometimes to the homes of the people involved took place between September 1974 and September 1975. It was after my initial visits and interviews in September 1974 with the purpose of writing a magazine article about the show that I found myself so enthralled and fascinated with what I had seen and learned that I wanted to turn the project into a book. I discussed this proposal with Mrs. Nixon in October, and she agreed to co-operate in the further research that would be necessary. The cast and production staff joined her in giving me their intelligent, gracious, and good-humored co-operation. It is a privilege to know them and a pleasure to have been among them.

I mention the dates because you should understand that because of the lengthy schedule of book production, you will naturally not be reading an account of current goings-on in Pine Valley as you see them on your television screen. Agnes Nixon was trusting and generous enough to tell me in May some "future story," a preciously guarded secret, so that I would at least have a notion of what would be happening in the story when my book would be born nine months later. (The birth of books takes the same length of time as the birth of children, and with much the same symptoms of anxiety and "morning sickness" on the part of author as well as mother.) But the book cannot depend on the plot of the televised story; rather, it must rely on what continuing interest there is in how a daytime television serial is created, produced, and acted, and how the lives of the "characters" sometimes flow into the "real lives" of the people who play them. To distinguish between actor and character, I have employed the simple device of printing the name of the character in italics and the name of the actor in regular type. This is necessary because, among other reasons, in the studio they are called by both names interchangeably; that is, someone may call Lawrence Keith by his own name of Larry or he may be called by his character's name, as in "We need *Nick Davis* on the set now."

For those who have not yet watched the show, I have made a list of the cast with a brief summary of the characters they play. Again, you must remember that this "character sketch" is based on their behavior and relationships as of September 1975, and by the time you read this many will have changed their spouses, their jobs, even perhaps undergone some changes in their personality. In a few cases a "personality change" will be due to the fact that the part is being played by a new actor.

So tune in tomorrow.

And in the meantime, turn the page. . . .

The Cast of "All My Children"

The Place   Pine Valley, U.S.A., a suburban community with a small-town flavor, about an hour's train ride from New York City, where people sometimes go for abortions or art-gallery tours.

The Martin Family

Kay Campbell   *Kate Martin,* wise and kindly All-American grandmother, who might well be the inventor of apple pie; mother of *Dr. Joe* and lawyer *Paul Martin,* grandmother of *Tara Martin Tyler* and *Jeff Martin,* great-grandmother of Tara's son, *Little Phillip Tyler.*

Ray MacDonnell   *Dr. Joe Martin,* the firm and good physician we think we had in childhood who always made house calls for head colds; father of *Tara* and *Jeff,* husband of *Ruth.*

Mary Fickett   Nurse *Ruth Martin,* the warm and appealing, steadfast and true woman whose shoulder you'd most like to cry on; wife of *Dr. Joe* and adoptive mother of *Phil Brent.*

Charles Frank   *Dr. Jeff Martin,* super-wholesome son of *Dr. Joe,* a sort of medical Pat Boone but still miraculously likable. Big brother of *Tara,* and husband of *Mary.*

Susan Blanchard   *Mary Kennicott Martin,* adoring wife of *Dr. Jeff,* devoted nurse, freckle-faced friend to all stray puppies of the world.

Matthew Anton   *Tad Martin,* abandoned child being raised by Grandma *Kate,* a precocious kid who is a big hit with adults.

William Mooney   Attorney *Paul Martin,* the soul of boyish sincerity whom every woman would want to handle her divorce; married currently to *Margo Flax Martin,* but still in love with his former wife, *Anne Tyler.*

Eileen Letchworth   *Margo Flax Martin,* a former model who secretly got a face lift to lure the young *Paul* into

marriage and does her yoga every day in a vain effort to
stay alluring to him. Time is not on her side.

The Tyler Family

Hugh Franklin   *Dr. Charles Tyler,* chief of staff of the Pine
Valley Hospital, could easily get a job as an Ivy League
college president; husband of *Phoebe,* father of *Anne* and
Lincoln, grandfather of *Chuck,* great-grandfather of
Little Phillip.

Ruth Warrick   *Phoebe Tyler,* wife of *Charles,* mother of
Lincoln and *Anne,* grandmother of *Chuck;* epitome of the
snobbish socialite, her heart belongs mainly to the Pine
Valley Country Club.

Judith Barcroft   *Anne Tyler,* lovely and wistful divorcée
who is trying temporarily to drown her sorrows in volunteer work for the Pine Valley Hospital.

Peter White   *Lincoln Tyler,* brother of *Anne Tyler,* suave
attorney with an appreciation of music and the arts and
also of *Kitty Shea,* who comes from across the tracks but
is eager to learn about music and the arts.

Chris Hubbell   *Dr. Chuck Tyler,* handsome young intern
who must have been social director of his Sigma Chi
chapter; was raised by his grandparents *Charles* and
Phoebe Tyler because his own parents had died when the
story began; husband of *Tara,* legal father of *Little
Phillip.*

Stephanie Braxton   *Tara Martin Tyler,* not fluffy enough to
be Sweetheart of Sigma Chi, but properly appealing
enough for all the Brothers to want to marry; sister of *Jeff
Martin,* mother of *Little Phillip,* who is really the natural
son of *Phil Brent,* who is *Tara's* first love and *Chuck's*
best friend.

Ian Washam   *Little Phillip Tyler,* curly-haired blond little
son of *Tara,* legal son of *Chuck* and natural son of *Phil,*
he is fortunately too young to have learned about these
complications yet.

Other Pine Valley Residents

Lawrence Keith   *Nick Davis*, originally a cad who ran the local dance studio, has now opened a nightclub-restaurant and is not only more respectable than he used to be but sometimes is a nice guy. Has been married to *Anne Tyler* and *Kitty Shea*, is the natural father of *Phil Brent*.

Nick Benedict   *Phil Brent*, a loser who is such a nice guy no one can figure out why he's such a loser. Returns from Vietnam to find his best girl married to his best friend, is laid off from his ecology job, gets *Erica Kane* pregnant and marries her, whereupon she has a miscarriage and a mental breakdown.

Susan Lucci   *Erica Kane Martin Brent*, the beautiful but bitchily neurotic *femme fatale* of Pine Valley who tries hard to be good but always blows it in the end.

Frances Heflin   *Mona Kane*, long-suffering mother of *Erica*, who pathetically believes her daughter will eventually turn out all right; also secretary to *Dr. Charles Tyler*, and his increasingly close friend. They prove romance has no age limit.

Francesca James   *Kitty Shea*, attractive and admirable young woman who has transformed herself from a doormat for *Nick* to a self-assured young lady engaged to marry *Lincoln Tyler*.

Paulette Breen   *Claudette Flax Montgomery*, sexy, spoiled-rotten daughter of *Margo*, who has recently come to Pine Valley after leaving her wealthy husband and is wreaking havoc right and left. She is going to give *Erica* a run for her money as the town bitch.

John Danelle   *Dr. Frank Grant*, intelligent, comforting young black man to whom people pour out their problems. His main role at Pine Valley has been to console people during coffee breaks, but by the time you read this he will be launched into his own crisis and will need some coffee breaks himself.

Avis McArthur   *Nancy Grant*, has hardly been seen at all

till now, but comes into prominence as her husband at last gets to have his own crisis. In fact she provides it for him. . . . (The part was originally played by Lisa Wilkinson, real-life wife of "Dr. Grant," who left the show for other theatrical commitments.)

Fred Porcelli   *Freddie,* the maître d' of the Château Nick Davis in Pine Valley; in real life trains for his role by serving as maître d' for the 21 Club in New York City.

Prologue

QUEEN AND HEIR

Imagine a young woman three days out of college who has sold a radio play while she still was a student, who was burning with desire and ambition to be a writer, a profession that was as difficult to make a living in then in 1946 as it was in Charles Dickens' time and is today and always has been and always will be. Imagine—and this should not be hard—that her father thinks her wish to be a writer is frivolous and unrealistic.

Our heroine, facing the grown-up world of work and wages, responsibilities and taxes, has only one job offer.

That is from her father.

He wants his daughter to come and work for him in his own business.

He is in the burial-garment business.

"Talk about inspiration," the daughter recalls many years later. "I just *had* to be successful at something to avoid being in the burial-garment business!"

The father cited a friend of his in the burial-garment business whose dutiful daughter had gladly gone to work for him, and this precedent seemed to the father to emphasize the sensibleness and rightness of his own daughter doing the same thing. But the daughter insisted she could make a living as a writer and she'd prove it if she just had the chance.

Hoping to show the obstinate daughter the impracticality of her ambition, the father said he would get her an interview with someone in the writing business, so she could learn for herself how inadequate she was for such a career. The father inquired among his friends, and one of them, a doctor, in fact knew a woman in the writing business. This was in Chicago, which was the birthplace of the popular daytime radio serials, or "soap operas," and many of those programs still originated from there.

So the ambitious daughter took along a script of a play she had written, and went to see the woman who was actually a professional Writer, who wrote four different daytime serials and hired other people to help her with the daily dialogue.

The daughter was naturally awed and frightened to meet the professional woman Writer, and even now she remembers that when the Writer asked to see the script she had written, and proceeded then to *read it out loud* while the young woman sat there and listened, "I was simply terrified."

When the Writer was finished reading the script she put it down beside her, looked at its young author, and asked, "Would you like to come to work for me?"

The question, and the obvious answer, are now a part of the history of the medium in which the two women worked.

The older writer who asked the question was Irna Phillips, who was known until almost the time of her death a few years ago as "the Queen of Soap Opera," and the younger writer, Agnes Eckhardt Nixon, was later to be regarded as "the Princess," "the Crown Princess of the Soaps," "the First Lady of Soap Opera," and "the heir apparent to Irna Phillips' crown."

As we know from fairy tales and other kinds of history, the Queen can be demanding, imperious, and difficult, and the relations of Queen and Princesses, especially those who are Heir Apparent, are likely to be especially difficult. So was this. And yet for all the difficulty there was an underlying respect and love, and many who knew the Queen say the Princess was one of the few people who was able to get along with her over a period of time. And it was almost a quarter of a century.

Irna Phillips was the Queen of her realm because she literally created it. Irna is to soap opera what Edison is to the light bulb and Fulton to the steamboat. There weren't any of these things before these people came along and invented them.

Growing up as a kid and listening to radio soap operas, I simply assumed they were a part of life and always had been, like Coca-Cola and comic books and Christmas and electric lights; I assumed all these things that were commonplaces of our existence had always been around, that when God created the earth he made not only the animals and birds and lakes and trees but also the electric lights and the radios and the programs you heard on them. (On the first day of creation, at 12:15 P.M. Central Standard Time, God must have said, "Let there be 'Ma Perkins,'" and lo, you turned the dial of your radio, and there was.)

Actually, this latter phenomenon was created just in time for me, 1932, the year I was born. Two years before that, Irna Phillips, who had graduated with an M.A. in drama from the University of Illinois and was working as a schoolteacher in Dayton, Ohio, specializing in "storytelling" and children's theater, went home to visit her family in Chicago, toured radio station WGN, was accidentally given a script to read, did so, and was offered a job. She went to work for the station doing a talk program called "Thoughts for the Day," and then wrote for the station a "family serial" called "Painted Dreams." Before that there had been a few nighttime serials like "Amos 'n' Andy," but they were a far cry from the daytime "family serial" that Irna created which set the style for the future flood of similar daily dramas soon to be known as soap operas.

Until then, radio had been filled with public service messages on health and hygiene, as well as the droning market reports, and a woman at home tuning into a local station was likely to hear an enthralling monotone recital of hog prices up one fourth, soybeans down an eighth, grain steady at five and a half. . . .

In the midst of that glum business, Irna gave them—*stories*. Others quickly followed; Elaine Carrington, and Frank and Ann Hummert, and there are claims as to who did most and more, for though Irna by the mid-thirties was writing or dictating 60,000 words a week for a total of something like 3 million words a year, statisticians have found that the Hummerts around the same time were churning out 6.5 million words a year! Of course there were two Hummerts and only one Irna, but everyone began to realize that these feats were too much, and started hiring writers to help them.

Irna hired the recently graduated Agnes Eckhardt to write dialogue for her program "A Woman in White."

Irna was the only one of the leading radio soap opera writers to make the transition to television and indeed to come to dominate the daytime serials of that medium. She brought some of her own radio soaps to TV, such as "The Guiding Light," and created new ones, such as "Another World" and "As the World Turns."

She dominated the medium until her death, and even beyond, according to some people who otherwise do not admit to a belief in the occult.

Mary Harris and Bud Kloss both worked for Irna during the days when radio soaps were being translated to television, and they are telling me about those times, which of course include a lot of Irna. Bud is now the producer of "All My Children" and Mary has left television to do editorial work for magazines of the Hearst Corporation, but they still keep in touch and every once in a while meet for a drink and talk about the old days. As an outsider interested in the era, I am asking them a lot of questions, and we find ourselves talking increasingly of Irna. Suddenly Mary puts her drink down with a decisive movement, as if for emphasis, and says,

"She's still here. Irna's *skeletal hand* is still directing the whole damn thing."

Although Irna has died about two years before this, I get the eerie feeling Mary is right, at least in the sense that no one in the business who knew Irna has yet stopped thinking or talking of her. As I interview people who work in this business, I get the feeling sometimes that Irna is looking over their shoulder.

And mine.

The fantasy of Irna directing things from the grave is a little more plausible when you realize that during her lifetime she directed her many programs from someplace almost as far away from where they were being produced: Chicago. By the fifties all the radio soaps had moved to New York, and all the TV soaps would soon be done either there or in Hollywood, and so all the actors and writers and producers and cameramen and technicians moved with them.

All except Irna.

Irna stayed in Chicago, and, with her telephone and her television set, and two or three train trips a year to New York, she ran, as it were, the whole show.

Especially with the telephone. She was an artist with the telephone, commanding and cajoling, directing and demanding, as she sat in her Chicago headquarters–command post, a Rommel-like strategist. Mary Harris recalls: "Her long suit was the telephone. She called you at all hours of the day and night. Every three months or so those of us who worked on 'Another World' would go to Chicago to meet with Irna, but in between, the main thing was the phone."

Bud: "I remember when Irna gave me the phone number not just of the room she worked in but the number of the phone in her bedroom. *That* was a real status symbol. I remember I told my boss she'd given me that number, and he nodded, and said, 'You're *in* now.'"

Bud smiles and says, "But it had its drawbacks. I remember once having people for dinner, and the phone rang. This was during the time I worked for Irna, for five years I was associate producer on her show 'Another World.' Well, as I was saying, the phone rang, and, like a fool, I answered it. Of course, it was Irna. I told her I was just about to sit down to dinner with guests and she said that was all right, it would only take a few minutes. The call took an hour and a half and when I finally sat down, the dinner was cold."

If there is frustration in these memories there is also fascination and admiration, as soldiers might talk about a demanding but winning general they served under and sometimes fought against.

"Sitting out there in Chicago, with only that telephone," Mary recalls, "she could call up actors and get them to work for her, get them from your show on to hers before you even knew about it."

Bud: "That's right. Irna always had the news first. She knew which actors were unhappy, which ones wanted to make a change—and not just actors on her own shows, but on other shows."

When I speak of my amazement at all the stories she kept going, all the balls juggling in the air at one time, Bud and Mary tell me how she used everything, absorbed everything, put it away in her mind and brought it out for story or dialogue.

Bud: "She used everything you told her, no matter how innocuous you tried to make it. Irna when she came to New York on the train was often met at the station by a young man pushing a wheelchair who would wheel her around. I was once that young man. I got her a cab and took her to her hotel and as we were driving there she asked me, 'What's going on in your life?' and I was immediately on guard, knowing how she used everything, and I said, 'Irna, my life's an open book.' A few months later I was watching 'Another World' and one of the characters says in response to that question, 'My life's an open book,' and the other person says, 'Lives whose books aren't quite open are more interesting.'"

Mary: "Yes, once my mother was ill and Irna asked what was wrong with her and I said the doctor had told me, 'When you get to a certain age, the machinery starts breaking down,' and some weeks later a character on 'Another World' is ill and asks the doctor what's wrong and he says, 'When you get to a certain age, the machinery starts breaking down.'"

I ask if she also used things from what she read, about

things going on in the world, from papers and magazines, etc., and Mary shakes her head and says:

"I never heard Irna say a word about public affairs or politics. As far as I know, the only two books she ever read were *You Can't Go Home Again* and *Profiles in Courage*. She loved *Profiles in Courage*, and mentioned it on her shows so much, having people refer to it admiringly, that the network got after her.

"Once I was with her in fall of '64 and we were watching TV and Goldwater came on the screen. She said, 'Who's that?' I said, 'That's Barry Goldwater.' She said, 'Who's he?' I said, 'Irna, he's the Republican party candidate for President.' She looked closer at the screen, and finally said, 'That's good casting.'

"I was in her apartment in Chicago when it had just been redone and there was a bookcase but it mostly had knick-knacks on it. There were only about twenty books in the whole place. Also she never had the kind of writing mess that most writers have, a lot of papers and all that. Her desk was always neat and clean. Of course, she didn't have to write; she could dictate a half-hour script in half an hour."

According to everyone I talked to about Irna, her genius included some idiosyncrasies, mainly a fear of and fascination for doctors and medicine and illness. She was moved around often by wheelchair and consulted a doctor or doctors every day or so. One of the great ironies of our popular culture is that almost every soap opera has at least one or more doctors on it and this has always been critically analyzed as a studied appeal to the interests of American housewives. In fact, the whole thing may have come about simply because of Irna Phillips' obsession with doctors and medicine. It was she who put the first doctor to work on a daytime serial, and maybe her own inclination matched that of the public, whose pulse she knew so expertly in her own role as drama doctor. . . .

Mary Harris remembers when word went around that Irna was going to sail to Europe, and many of those who had known her in the industry couldn't believe that this woman whose principal travel had been trains between New York and Chicago was going to really take a ship across the Atlantic Ocean to England. On the day she was to sail Mary and a friend who wrote TV serials were driving down the West Side Highway in Manhattan, and suddenly they broke out laughing. They saw, in dock, the hospital ship *Hope*. They figured Irna was indeed sailing to Europe, and had chosen just the right ship.

"I always wanted," Bud says, "to write a Broadway musical about Irna. The way I envisioned it, the stage would be split in two. On one half you'd see life as it was presented in Irna's programs, and on the other half you'd see Irna's life as it really was."

Irna was one of ten children of a Jewish family from Chicago, and the main character of her first serial, "Painted Dreams," was the Irish mother of a large family, the kindly Mother Monahan. Friends say Mother Monahan was modeled on her own mother, that her mother was the source of inspiration for many of her characters, and, as a typically appreciative article in the Chicago *Tribune* noted, "From 'Painted Dreams' to 'As the World Turns,' the home and family have been the core of Miss Phillips' radio and TV scripts."

In the first of her scripts, "Painted Dreams," Mother Monahan's daughter complained that a wedding ring would interfere with "the realization of the dream I've been painting all my life." And Mother Monahan warns that "when you're paintin' your dreams, be careful of the colors you're goin' to be usin', 'cause sometimes you make a mistake, and the colors that you think are goin' to look good don't look so good in the finished picture. Now, Frances, darlin', let me be sayin' just one more thing to ya. There are three colors that have stood the test of time. They are the colors that are the foundations of all the dreams of all men and women in the world—the colors of love . . . family . . . home." Mother Monahan elaborated these guidelines to a feminist character by saying, "In your plan, women wouldn't be havin' time to be havin' children and keepin' a home. . . . I'm thinkin' that a country is only as strong as its weakest home. When you're after destroyin' those things, which make up a home, you're destroyin' people."

Irna herself never married.

At age forty she adopted two children. She was a shrewd businesswoman, a brilliant careerist, whose work espoused and championed the cause of the woman as wife, mother, and homemaker.

Toward the end of her career Irna wrote a soap opera about a woman like herself. The heroine was a soap opera writer who lived in Chicago. It was called "A World Apart." It lasted barely a year.

Bud says it died because it violated every one of her own principles for soap opera.

Perhaps the two worlds of Irna's life could not be dramatically reconciled—at least not without the device of a split stage or split screen.

But however great the irony of Irna's split-screen life, she was still, by any measure, by any judgment of friend or foe, the Queen of the form of entertainment she created and carried from radio to television for an unbroken span of forty years.

On Christmas Day, in 1973, Agnes Nixon called Irna to wish her a happy holiday, and was told that Miss Phillips was dead. Miss Phillips had not wanted anyone to be informed of the event.

One of Agnes' fondest memories of Irna Phillips goes back to that time when Irna had hired her to work as a "dialogist" on one of her programs, "A Woman in White." Agnes' father had of course thought the interview with a professional writer would properly disabuse his daughter of her silly daydreams. When he heard that the writer had actually given Agnes a job that paid money to write stories for the radio, at first he couldn't believe it and then he reconciled the otherwise unexplainable matter by assuming that the whole thing was due to his own influence. When Mr. Eckhardt later encountered Miss Phillips in a doctor's office he said he wanted to thank her for the "favor" she had done his daughter.

Irna Phillips drew herself up to her full imperial psychic and physical stature and assured Mr. Eckhardt in no uncertain terms that she had not done his daughter or anyone else any "favor."

"Sir," said Irna Phillips in her grandest manner, *"I am a businesswoman!"* She added: "I hired your daughter because she will do a good job for me."

Agnes worked for, and learned from, Irna for six months before deciding for personal reasons, which included the increasing discomfort and distress of her father over her life as a writer and independent (from him) career woman, that she had best move on to New York. It was not only the logical but the ideal place for an ambitious young dramatic writer with experience in radio, for many of the radio daytime serials were moving there and also this was—as later recognized of course—"the Golden Age of Television," the brief and bountiful era of live and original drama on prime-time TV, and the field was wide open and exciting.

When I speak of this time with Agnes something more than twenty years later, in the comfort of her living room on a cold winter evening in front of a warm fireplace, I say I imagine that when she made that move Irna knew a lot of influential people in New York and provided her with helpful contacts.

Agnes folds her hands in her lap, and says with unusual precision, "Those are two different questions. The answer to one is, Yes, Irna knew a lot of influential people in New York. The answer to the other is, No, she did not put me in touch with them."

When Agnes arrived in New York her professional as well as social salvation at first was—"the Chicago people."

One of the great American traditions is for the young people from the provinces to come to New York and to seek out and find there, in the midst of all that success and confusion, their fellow intruders, allied outsiders, people whose speech and accent and background match their own and make them feel at home. I know because I was part of the syndrome,

finding in New York when I got out of college a surprising
and relieving number of other "Indiana people." My first job
after college was given to me by Barney Kilgore, a native of
South Bend, Indiana, graduate of DePauw University in
Greencastle, Indiana, and when I met him with my frail
packet of clippings he was publisher of the *Wall Street Journal*, but still very proudly and pointedly one of the Indiana
people. He swung around in his swivel chair and said, "Well,
you bein' from Indiana, you'll do all right here. These New
York fellas, they don't do so good."

Agnes found a ready-made home among some Chicago people whose nucleus was the cast of the "Ma Perkins" radio program. The show had moved from Chicago in 1946 because, as
Ma herself (Virginia Payne) explains it, "Everyone was moving either East or West, everyone in show business, and both
New York and Hollywood wanted us and we chose New York.
It had become difficult to cast in Chicago, to find good people
for the right parts. The good actors were going either East or
West. You've heard of Chicago as the Second City? Well, it
still holds true. It's a wonderful starting place—very creative
people have come out of there and still do but then they have
to make that move East or West for the sake of their careers."

Agnes had met Ginny Payne back in Chicago when Ginny
as an actress and Agnes as a writer were doing some free-
lance work for a patriotic inspirational radio series called
"Freedom of Opportunity," a series of biographical dramas on
the lives of Great Americans. Agnes had got an assignment to
write one on Mr. Hershey, the chocolate-bar maker, and
Ginny was playing the role of his "steadfast wife, Lenore."
Agnes still remembers rehearsing for the program, and she
and Ginny trying not to break out giggling over the inspirational role of the steadfast wife, Lenore. To relieve the monot-
ony of the deadly righteous spirit of the enterprise, Agnes
wrote in a quick scene in which steadfast Lenore, while stir-
ring the vat of chocolate, dropped something into it by mistake and exclaimed, "Oh, nuts!" thus giving Mr. Hershey the
idea for making the first chocolate bar with nuts in it! Agnes
adds to the recollection, "Everyone cracked up—no one but

Ginny and I realized it was a put-on till we were halfway through the scene, but nobody minded, they just went back and redid it—that's how easy and casual things were then."

When Agnes got to New York she looked up Ginny, who offered her not only friendship but an introduction to Max Wylie, a brother of the novelist Philip Wylie, who worked for Young and Rubicam, and through his connections at the ad agency he put Agnes in touch with people at CBS, where she got her first free-lance work in New York.

"I was eking out a living, and I was lonely, and I hung around with Ginny and the other 'Ma Perkins' people. Ginny Payne and Kay Campbell, who used to be daughter Effie on 'Ma Perkins' and now is Grandma *Kate* on 'All My Children,' shared an apartment, and they took me under their wing. They used to go to the studio at eleven-thirty in the morning and they'd be done at one-thirty—that's how it was in those days—and I'd go over and have lunch with them."

At my own lunch with these grand ladies, Ginny and Kay, who still are friends, I recall Agnes' saying that, and Kay says, "Oh yes, Aggie came and had lunch with us all the time at the New Weston, and Ginny and I went over to see her in this little basement apartment she had. Oh Lord, but we worried about her! Such a young little thing, and alone in New York. We just wanted to hug her and protect her."

Ginny is nodding agreement and says, "We were very fond of her—and glad to have her here professionally, too. There weren't that many people who could write."

"And oh, did that girl work," Kay says. "She worked like a little Trojan. And she's wonderful to work *for*. I remember when I was asked to do a part on 'The Guiding Light' on television, and I said, 'I'm sorry, but I can't work for Irna Phillips. I'm scared of her. I really am.' They said, 'Well, don't worry then, because Irna's not writing it any more. Agnes Eckhardt's the writer.' And I brightened up and said, 'In that case, everything's fine.' Irna was big, though, she was a giant. Why, I tell you, Irna was so big that she told Procter and Gamble what to do—*and they did it!*

"But still, working for her—I'll never forget once on 'As the

World Turns,' Rosemary Prinz did a scene and when we were only off the air five minutes Irna was on the phone and tore her to pieces. I don't think Irna liked actors."

Ginny: "I don't either. But then I think a lot of authors resent actors."

Kay: "But Agnes has never been like that."

Ginny: "No, not Agnes."

A young man-about-town of that era working his way up in the magazine and publishing business sometimes went on double dates with a buddy who was squiring this new girl around and he remembers Agnes not so much with motherly concern as gentlemanly admiration. "What was she like then?" I asked him, and he said with genuine nostalgic enthusiasm, "Agnes was marvelous. A charming, lively little girl fresh out of Northwestern. She was slim, with reddish-blond hair, and a wonderful smile. She was fun to be around, and I don't mean just as a giggly attractive little girl. I mean she was *sharp*."

Indeed she must have been, for before long she was selling original dramas to the most prestigious live television shows of that time—or, it turns out, of any time—"Studio One," "Robert Montgomery Presents," "Somerset Maugham Theater," "Philco Theater," and "Hallmark Theater."

"You had to write an hour show and they didn't have tape in those days. It was all live—it was exciting, wild," says Agnes. (Bud Kloss and Mary Harris also told me that the days of live TV were more exhilarating, that the knowledge that any mistake would be seen, that there was no chance to go back and make a correction as there is now on "live tape" if a really bad goof is made, added to the adrenaline of everyone involved and to the drama of the production.)

But in the midst of this excitement of live TV and New York City, of being young and talented in the right time and place, Agnes got a call from a woman in Iowa, "a woman who has been a big influence in my life," a woman named Kate— much like the wise and kindly grandmother on her "All My Children" program. Agnes' own Irish maternal grandmother was named Kate, and this other Kate out in Iowa was also

Irish and like an "adopted mother" to Agnes. This Kate said
there is a young man she thinks Agnes ought to meet. His
name is Bob Nixon and he is working in Washington, D.C.,
for the Chrysler Corporation. He too believed in the wisdom
of Kate, and so he made a special trip up to New York to meet
Agnes. Four months later they were married. They are still
married now, twenty-four years later, and have four grown
children.

"So you can see why I believe in the Irish wisdom of grand-
mothers and mothers named Kate," Agnes says.

Agnes told an interviewer when her kids were growing up
that "when I was young and growing up in Nashville, this
kind of life [family and children] seemed so confining. . . .
I didn't want to be 'just a housewife' like the other girls I
knew."

Agnes became a housewife, but not "just." Soon after she
was married and her husband, Bob, was transferred to Philadelphia, she realized it would be difficult to write for those
live dramatic shows she'd been doing in New York, with most
of them moving to the West Coast, but she was not about to
give up her writing.

"Shortly after I was married, Irna asked me to come back."
In spite of the coolness between them when Agnes left
Chicago and went off on her own to New York, she and Irna
had got back in touch and kept in touch, and now, with the
Princess in a kind of geographic exile from her medium, the
Queen had asked her to return—not to Chicago but to work on
one of Irna's serials called "The Guiding Light."

"I did dialoguing on 'The Guiding Light,' and Irna and I
worked together completely by mail and by telephone, except
for a few times a year when she came into New York and I'd
go in to have dinner with her. After a while, when Irna was
busy with other programs, Procter and Gamble asked me to
be the head writer for 'The Guiding Light.' I felt it was a good
opportunity. The program was still only fifteen minutes a day,
the kids were still really small, and I was learning the craft."

For the past twenty years Agnes has written one or more
daytime serials five days a week, fifty-two weeks a year. With

a home and family people wondered how she did it—and some of them of course were raising their eyebrows and wagging their fingers, wondering if she didn't have to slight some part of her life to do all that writing. She did, but it wasn't her family.

"When the children were small," Agnes remembers, "I was writing and changing diapers too—I've had to give up the bridge clubs, the ladies' luncheons, the civic work—the only thing I've done like that is go to PTA or go see my son and daughters in school sports. Early on, a lot of people felt I couldn't be a good mother. Now of course the whole women's lib thing has exploded and a lot of attitudes like that have changed. Now there are women with a lot of free time who wish they were doing something. Now I get asked to speak at those women's clubs that fifteen years ago would have disapproved of what I was doing."

What she was doing was first really recognized in her own profession when she took over a serial called "Another World" that had slipped badly in the ratings, and with new plot and characters brought it up to Number Two.

A telegram from a Procter and Gamble executive said: "Congratulations on the 38.6 share and being the number 2 daytime show in the high cotton. . . ."

With that success behind her, Agnes was asked by ABC to do the most difficult and demanding job in her business. She was asked to "create her own show."

It was called "One Life to Live," and soon became a hit.

Perhaps the most personally important of the many accolades her own show received was a telegram in July 1968 that read: "Dear Aggie even though we are worlds and networks apart best to you in your new world."

That was from Irna.

Act I

INSIDE
THE STUDIO

After the success of her first "creation" Agnes Nixon has gone on to create another daytime TV serial, one that turns out to be her own favorite and the favorite of millions of devoted fans. This one is "All My Children."

Agnes doesn't often go on the set of the show but she knows what goes on there. I don't just mean among the people, though she knows that too, but what goes on in the production of the program, how it all works, how it is put together.

She is explaining the rigorous daily production schedule to a group of Philadelphia high school students who are listening with rapt attention, their eyes and ears and in some cases their mouths open in fascination. . . .

"The actors get their scripts three or four days ahead, and they tape the program one week before air time. That taping itself is something I think is very interesting because it shows what a really professional cast we have. I think this is the most difficult work in show business.

"They memorize their lines; they really do. If you ever catch them going to the TelePrompTers—you can tell when someone says, 'Well, excuse me,' and they look away from the camera—you know they're looking for the TelePrompTer. But anyone who does that too much is really looked down on by their peer group, and it's fabulous how well they can memorize their lines."

"The actors go in to the studio at eight o'clock in the morning and they have a 'line rehearsal' from eight to nine forty-five. During that time they sit on folding chairs and read their lines for interpretation and timing. The director sits with a stopwatch and, he will say, 'All right now, Mary, wait now. At this point you will be walking over to the fireplace and looking at *Phillip's* picture and then walking back, so let's allow time for that. All right, now your line.'

"The director, the night before, has sat down with his script and 'blocked' it, has written in every move he wants the actors to make, in addition to every camera shot that he wants taken. So he goes through that with the actors, perhaps they go through the script about three times, and then they go down to the floor of the studio, and they block, that is, they chart their movements, where they'll be walking to and from and where they'll be standing when they say a certain line.

"The director will say, 'Walk now, Mary—O.K., take three steps to the mantel, look at the picture, and turn back. Now. Deliver your line.' Mary knows this is what she's supposed to do by now, so she can do it without the director telling her, but the director is saying it over the microphone that is connected to the earpieces which the cameramen and the technical director on the floor have, and the lighting director and the sound director and the music director. They all have these headpieces so that they hear the director saying, 'O.K., when Mary is looking at the picture above the fireplace, move in for a tight shot on Camera Two; Camera Three, be ready to take *Phil* as she walks over to him.'

"And while these things are going on the lighting director has to control the lights and make sure there's light on the picture when Mary looks at it, that another light is ready to pick up her face as she turns back. And the sound technician is moving the boom to the right place to pick up her voice. Maybe you've seen the sound boom—sometimes the camera goofs and you see it on the screen, a long boom with a microphone that hangs on the end of it. Well, the sound technician is moving that constantly, and not only does he have to make sure he's picking up their voices, he has to make sure he doesn't hit them on the head at the same time. Really, it's very tricky. I'm constantly amazed at how they can do all these things at once, keep everything in mind and get it all done.

"After the blocking, supposedly there's lunch from eleven to twelve-fifteen, but don't let that fool you. Maybe all the men have lunch, but most of the ladies are running to get their hair done and get into their makeup. It's a wild time, and most likely while the hairdresser is doing something to their hair they're eating a sandwich and drinking a malted, and that's about what lunch consists of.

"At twelve-fifteen to twelve forty-five they do a runthrough, which is with all the sets and furniture, and with everybody working in concert, director and actors and technical people. After that, the director gets together with the cast and gives his 'Notes.' All day he and his assistants have made notes about problems or suggestions or changes, about everything from interpretations of lines to changes of positioning on the set.

"At one-fifteen to one forty-five there's a dress rehearsal, which means with makeup, right straight through, and no stops unless somebody really makes a terrible goof or a piece of scenery falls down or someone gets hit on the head. And after the dress rehearsal the director gives Notes again, and, in addition to everything else, if at this point the script turns out to be a little too long they have to make cuts in the dialogue, which means that without ever having another rehearsal, those actors whose speech has been shortened just keep that in mind and make that jump to the other line. And I think that in itself is fabulous, the way they can do that.

"From two-fifteen to two forty-five is taping, and again if there's some horrible goof we stop and retape a segment, but we don't have much leeway in time, because we have to be out of the studio by four-thirty because the evening news program comes in and sets up then, so we don't have the luxury of just going on and on, redoing things. And then the tape is checked, and everyone has to wait to see if it's all right.

"If the tape hasn't broken, if there aren't any blank spots on the tape, if the tape machine didn't konk out, then after that, which is now about three or three-thirty, the actors can go home, and believe me, by that time, the way the adrenaline's been flowing, it's been an exhausting day. And when the actors go home many of them have to memorize *another* half-hour script for the *next* day. The director has to block his show and come back the next morning at eight o'clock. We do have two directors, so one directs three shows in a row, then the other does the next three, and of course we certainly try not to use our actors five days a week every week, but there are times when they're on five, six, and seven shows in a row, and it's really physically punishing, they really have to be in training. An actor on a serial compared to a movie actor is like a long-distance runner as opposed to a javelin thrower; our actors just have to keep in shape, you know, to do it."

I am nodding in vigorous agreement, for even though I'm not an actor I've found that just sitting around the studio and *watching* the rehearsals and production of a show from eight in the morning till sometime past three in the afternoon is an exhausting experience. I find that on the days I go to the studio I do not try to do any interviews after I leave at three but instead return to my hotel, take off my shoes, flop on the bed, and try to get up the strength to take a shower. It's sort of like spending a day watching your favorite pro football team work out, except the exhaustion you share with your heroes of soapland is from emotional and mental rather than physical punishment.

The first day I visit the set of "All My Children" happens to be by accident a kind of special occasion.

It is the first day that the actress Eileen Letchworth is to make an appearance as the character *Margo* after she has had her face lift.

I may have already confused you by saying "after she has

had her face lift" when I have just mentioned Eileen the actress or "real person" and *Margo* the character in the program. But this is a confusion that we must become aware of, if perhaps never quite accustomed to, because there is so often an overlapping of the two *personae* in the program. The face lift of Eileen/*Margo* is a case in point.

Eileen Letchworth is an actress who has decided for professional reasons it would be advantageous to have what is called "cosmetic surgery" of the variety commonly known as a "face lift" so that she will be able to play roles of younger women for a longer time. In order to have the operation she has to request time off from her role in "All My Children" and explain the reason for her desired leave of absence. When Agnes Nixon hears that Eileen wants to have a face lift she talks to her about it, and during their discussion Eileen has the idea that the whole experience might be worked into the *story*. Agnes likes to build stories around real issues that people experience in contemporary times, and it seemed a natural and instructive theme to use. Eileen was eager to co-operate in having her own personal experience built into the story of the character she played.

Agnes had time to develop the story of *Margo* falling in love with a man a little younger than herself, the handsome lawyer *Paul Martin,* and weave into this an all-out effort by *Margo* to become more attractive to *Paul* by pretending to leave town in order to visit her young married daughter in Newport, Rhode Island, during the summer, while in fact she goes to New York and has the face-lift operation.

When *Margo* returns to Pine Valley from New York after the operation, she is naturally anxious about the effect it will have on her beloved *Paul*. She wants him to find her more attractive, and yet she doesn't want him to know she has had a face lift.

She hopes he will simply believe that her general physical demeanor has been improved by her vacation with daughter and son-in-law in the fashionable summer resort of Newport. Naturally, before confronting *Paul* face-to—uh, as it were— face lift, she wants to check out her appearance with a trusted woman friend, and so, in today's episode, *Margo* has coffee at a restaurant with her trusted older woman friend *Mona Kane*, to get a friendly but frank appraisal of how she looks after her operation. Naturally *Margo* is nervous.

So is Eileen.

Part of the story has been to show *Margo* before her operation, have her express her fears to the surgeon, have him give her factual explanations and reassurances about the operation, and to show her after it is over when she is still in her bandages. But this will be the first time she will be shown full-face on camera. Either *Margo* or Eileen.

Margo is worried about what *Mona* will think about how she looks and how *Paul* will react.

Eileen is worried about how the camera will show her, and how ten million viewers will react.

It is only a small scene, a brief part of the many threads of the story line being filmed today. It is played on what is called a "half set," a small backdrop with a restaurant booth where two women, *Margo* and *Mona*, sit having coffee. *Margo* is wearing a scarf around her head. *Mona* says she looks fine but *Margo* says she doesn't really know yet, she hasn't seen all of her face yet. Dramatically—and this is one hell of a dramatic scene in the long unrolling of the story, somewhat like those moments in movies when the dancer tries to stand for the first time after a leg operation, or the Count of Monte Cristo takes off his mask—*Margo* removes her scarf, and tilts her chin up.

There is the appropriate pause, hush, and *Mona* says, "Oh—*Margo*—you look *wonderful!*"

And the audience breathes a sigh of relief.

Eileen can't. Not yet. She hasn't yet seen how it looks on camera. Her and *Margo's* face lift.

After the taping, producer Bud Kloss asks that this scene be shown again, and Eileen is back in the console room, and some of the other cast members are there to see too, in fact they are crowded in.

The moment comes. The scarf is removed. *Margo*/Eileen's

face—lifted—is revealed in a close-up on the full-color monitor screen.

There are oohs and aahs of approval.

Charlie Frank/*Jeff Martin* says, "Hey, who's the teen-ager!"

Mary Fickett/nurse *Ruth* says how beautiful she looks.

Eileen begins to smile. She looks at Bud Kloss to her right and Del Hughes the director to her left and says, "Hey, I feel like I'm sitting between a couple of older *men.*"

There are laughs and whistles. Eileen says, "You guys are all too old for me now."

Charlie Frank says the only man in the cast young enough for her is *Tad,* a ten-year-old boy played by Matthew Anton.

Everyone laughs, friendly. Eileen grins, relieved.

The others disperse and Bud invites me to come back with him to Eileen's dressing room, where she is to be photographed for a cover picture for one of the soap opera fan magazines called *Daytime TV Stars.*

The small room has a dressing table with a large mirror, and light-blue walls. There is a copy of *Daytime TV Stars* on the dressing table and there is also a pile of "get well" cards from fans, expressing concern about the face lift. Some of the cards are addressed to Eileen. Some are addressed to *Margo.*

The photographer from *Daytime TV,* Alan Rosenberg, has taken pictures of Eileen *before* the face lift and now he wants to take the *after* picture.

"You look wonderful," he tells her as he starts snapping photos. "This is going to be a terrific feature. The before and after shots."

"But you have to remember," Eileen says, looking worried for a moment, "this is only five weeks after the operation. The way I am now. That's not full recovery."

Snap, snap.

"Would you turn that way, please?" Rosenberg asks.

Eileen turns, tilting her chin.

"So you ought to be sure to say that this is only how it is after five weeks," she says.

Bud says, "Yes, you should put that in the caption—that it's only five weeks."

Snap, snap.

"You really are courageous, to do this publicly," Rosenberg says, bending and focusing and snapping.

Eileen tilts her head and says, "I hope it will help other women not to be ashamed of having this type of operation or afraid of having it done. I hope they won't be afraid to have a chin lift, or a nose job or anything else, if that's what they want to do."

Eileen touches a finger to her nose.

"My own surgeon, who did the operation, is just dying to do my nose now. He says he'll even do it free."

She looks in the mirror, bending her head slightly forward as Rosenberg continues to shoot.

"Frankly," Eileen says, "I don't see anything wrong with my nose. A lot of people seem to think it's funny or something, but it seems O.K. to me."

It seems O.K. to me, too, but I don't think it's my place to say anything. Besides, I can already imagine a whole lot of story lines around it. What if, for instance, lawyer *Paul* tells *Margo* he likes her a lot, but that he frankly has always felt that—well, her nose—something about it seemed odd . . . ? Or what if Eileen's surgeon's desire to work on her nose, for free, convinced her it might be a good idea, and then maybe it could be worked into the story so that lawyer *Paul* could say . . . ?

Rosenberg finishes and I follow Bud back up to his office where Frances Heflin (known to her friends as Fra), who plays *Mona,* is waiting to see him, and I wonder if it has anything to do with Eileen/*Margo* and her face lift. In fact it is about a cosmetic problem, but a far less drastic one. Fra says she's worried because her eyes have been very watery the past few days and she wonders if it's showing up on camera and if so whether she should do anything about it. Bud assures her it's all right; it's nothing to worry about.

"There's a very high pollen count right now, that's probably what's causing it," he says. "And it doesn't show on camera at all."

"Oh, I'm glad," Fra says.

She smiles. Relieved.

Bud goes into his office. There are phone calls that must be returned.

Every weekday from eleven until noon Bud Kloss, the producer of "All My Children," has lunch in a back booth in McGlade's. McGlade's is a pleasantly old-fashioned bar and grill with red-checkered tablecloths that is just across the street from the ABC–TV studios on Manhattan's West Sixty-seventh Street where both "All My Children" and "One Life to Live" are produced.

When I go to meet Bud there for what shall be the first of many pleasant and informative visits, I arrive a little early. At eleven, there aren't too many customers, and I look around the place, examining an impressive bronze bust with an inscribed plaque that reads: "Patrick McGlade—Humanitarian, Publican, Leprechaun—from his many friends—March 1969." McGlade's is not one of your newfangled, hip sort of places. McGlade's is *traditional*. The walls are wood-paneled, the lighting is dim, and when the afternoon sun comes in through the front windows, dust motes slowly spiral in the slanting beams. McGlade's is a comforting sort of place.

I sit down and tell a waiter I don't want to order anything yet; I'm waiting for Mr. Kloss.

"Ah," says the waiter. "Then you're in the wrong booth, sir. Mr. Kloss's booth is back here. The one with the light."

They have rigged up a small brass lamp over this booth in the back where Bud likes to sit so he can read without trouble the day's correspondence and business papers. For lunch Bud has one manhattan, straight up, and after he finishes sipping it he orders one of the day's specials from the home-typed piece of paper affixed inside the aged menu with a paper clip.

Bud has fairly close-cropped black hair, black-rimmed glasses with a band that allows them to hang down over his chest when he isn't using them, and he is wearing gray slacks and a navy-blue jacket, a crisp white shirt and a thin polka-dot tie. He is trim, in appearance and speech, and has a wry good sense of humor and an obvious enjoyment of his work. I order a white wine while Bud has his manhattan, and he tells me how he got into this business.

After graduating from Columbia College, Bud worked in advertising in the early fifties, with Young and Rubicam, and was first assigned to the Modess account. "We did three TV commercials with the theme line 'Modess Because—' and they were pulled off the air due to the angry reaction of women viewers. The ladies said, 'How dare you—talk about such things on the air!' That's how much attitudes have changed. Now we've even had commercials for a douche—a few of our own ladies on the show fell to the floor when they first saw that one.

"Anyway I became a representative of the television department of Y & R, to see that the shows their clients sponsored were acceptable to the clients—the job was known informally in the industry as being an 'agency fink.' Through my contacts with the TV industry, I wound up working on daytime television, and got to be associate producer of 'Another World.' I came to 'All My Children' when it first started in January 1970.

"When I talk about attitudes changing, daytime TV used to be considered strictly a woman's world—anything the ladies out there discussed with each other was O.K. Otherwise, not. That's changed enormously. We've had story lines on abortion, on the Vietnam War, on male sterility. . . . If we feel a subject we haven't done before fits into our story we back it up; we go to the network and fight for it.

"Daytime has much more freedom than people believe— especially people who put down soap opera without ever watching the shows. Daytime also has some of the best actors in the country. As best we can, we try to work things around the personal needs of the cast—if they want to take a long weekend, or be in an out-of-town production, we try to accommodate them. The important thing is to keep the group happy, otherwise the whole thing doesn't work."

Bud says he was on the phone to Agnes three different times this morning about different production problems and I ask what they are, what kind of things he and Agnes discuss. "Details," he says.

"For example, once today we were talking about what kind of wedding dress *Erica* should have. She's been married before, to *Dr. Jeff Martin,* so she wouldn't wear white. Also, since the divorce she's been sleeping around. So we don't want a traditional wedding gown, but we've got to have one that's true to *Erica's* type, one that will fit her image. Also one that will fit *her,* and that's another problem because Susan is a very small size."

Details.

More details are waiting when Bud returns at noon to the studio. The door between the control room and the studio is stuck, and it has to close by the time the show is taped. Henry Kaplan, the director for this day's program, is late getting back because he got something stuck in his throat at breakfast and had to see a doctor during his lunch break. Stephanie Braxton has her hair in two long braids for a breakfast scene in *Tara's* kitchen and Bud tells her he doesn't think it's the sort of thing *Tara* would wear; it makes her look as if she's a lady of leisure who has all the time in the world to make herself up in the morning, instead of a regular young housewife and mother whom people can identify with. Stephanie says actually it only takes about two and a half minutes to braid her hair in that fashion and Bud says nevertheless it *looks* like it took a lot of time and preparation and Stephanie says O.K. then, and starts unbraiding. A production assistant tells Bud there's a tree branch on the set of the *Martin* family patio that sticks out over *Ruth Martin's* face in a crucial scene, and Bud walks briskly onto the set and breaks off the offending branch. There is a moan from one of the cameramen. "What's wrong?" Bud asks. "I *loved* that branch," the cameraman says.

Details.

One of Mary Fickett's many fan letters compliments her because, among her other virtues as the actress playing the role of the understanding, loyal, attractive, intelligent, kindly nurse *Ruth Martin,* "you cry so good."

Mary is crying again.

As usual, she is doing it "good."

She is taping the last scene of the day's program, in which she has an emotional argument with her husband, the staunch and steadfast *Dr. Joe Martin,* played by Ray MacDonnell, and it is as good and convincing and moving a scene as I can remember seeing in any movie or theater performance in recent memory. Some of the day's other cast members who have finished their scenes are watching on the monitor, as transfixed as I am. Judith Barcroft is intently sipping a large Coke through a straw, Chris Hubbell is leaning forward in his seat, and Kay Campbell is standing just beside and a little behind director Henry Kaplan, her hands knotted tightly in front of her. When Henry signals the end of the scene, he turns to look at Kay and says, "My God, she's crying again! You've got to stop that!" and he pulls her toward him with a hug and Kay, sniffling, says, "Oh Lord. I even get weepy at the crawl, when they play the theme music."

But she is not the only one moved by Mary's good crying. The others, if not weepy, are impressed, and when Mary comes in off the set they congratulate her. Mary thanks them, flops down in one of the swivel chairs, and says, "My God, I'm exhausted. I feel like Bette Davis or something."

The scene she has just played here for a soap opera is as demanding as those she has played in movies and theater and nighttime television dramas. She has won the Theatre Guild Award and a Tony nomination for her portrayal of Eleanor Roosevelt in *Sunrise at Campobello* on Broadway; she understudied Deborah Kerr and Joan Fontaine for the lead in *Tea and Sympathy* and when she finally took over the role won the Theater World Award for most promising newcomer of the Broadway season. Perhaps because she brings the same talent and professionalism to her role as nurse *Ruth* as she has to her other more theatrically prestigious work, she is the first soap opera performer to win an Emmy award, given to her by the Television Academy in 1973 for "individual achievement in daytime drama."

Right now she is slumped in a chair in her *Ruth Martin* nurse's uniform and she says, "I'd like to sleep for three hours." Henry Kaplan, who is given to kidding around and shouting a lot, turns to her and says very quietly, "Mary, that was fine," and she smiles and, with equally sincere professional appreciation, says, "Thank you."

I have an appointment to talk with her after the taping is done, but now, seeing how genuinely exhausted she is, I ask her if she still wants to do it; we can talk another time if she's feeling too tired now, but she perks up and says no, this is fine, she just wants to change.

She emerges from her dressing room about ten minutes later wearing a soft yellow sweater and matching slacks, and the warm, cheery tone of her outfit matches her mood. If doing the scene was exhausting, its success and the response to it are exhilarating. Mary is glowing. I suggest that instead of sitting in some antiseptic office we go across the street and have a—well, an iced tea, while we talk. It is around three-thirty in the afternoon, and I can't imagine nurse *Ruth Martin* having a drink at such an hour, and I don't want her to think that I'm the sort of dissolute person who would suggest such a thing. I want her to think I'm a real swell guy. Not just because like most people I'd rather be liked than disliked, but I feel that if nurse *Ruth Martin* doesn't like me there must be something wrong; I must have failed in some basic way to be a worthy and virtuous human being.

When we go outside I hear a voice say, "There's *Ruth!*" and I look around and see a half dozen or so young women, smiling, waiting on the sidewalk to see—well, not the actors so much as the citizens of Pine Valley. They are not greeting Mary Fickett but nurse *Ruth Martin,* as they wave now and say, "Hi, *Ruth,*" "Good luck, *Ruth,*" and Mary waves back and says, "Hi, hello there!"

I straighten my tie, aware of my responsibility to look like a person fit to be escorting *Ruth Martin* across the street.

We take a table by the window at McGlade's and Mary

thinks iced tea is a good idea and we both have one. I tell her I am impressed not only by her performance but by the genuine way that the director and the other cast members responded to it also. I explain that although I am a true fan of the show I am imbued with the general notion that even though the audience may love their favorite soap operas, perhaps the people who work in them don't take them seriously except as a good way to make a living. In fact I know this is true in some cases, but it had seemed in this particular performance today there was a real and respectful appreciation of what she'd done.

She says that is true, at least on this program, not only among the other actors.

"After that scene," she says, "some of the stage crew complimented me, too. I think the success of this show, the feeling of it, is one of those chemical things that can occur. We happen to be a compatible group of people who enjoy one another and enjoy working together. When people from the outside ask me what it's like being on a soap opera—and the way they ask you can tell they assume it must be an awful chore, or boring or something—I say, 'Listen, if you have a job where you can start work at eight o'clock in the morning and be able to get a real belly laugh before nine, it can't be all bad. In fact, it must be something special.'"

I knew what she meant because I had been there in the bleak audition room at eight that morning when the actors for the day's program assemble to start running through their lines and, in these early run-throughs, relieve the tedium by clowning around. I watched Mary rehearse the scene that was later to be so dramatically effective in the taping for the actual broadcast, and heard her doing the lines with Ray Mac-Donnell, her stern and just husband, *Dr. Joe Martin*. Ray had a heavy line about how she must never disclose the secret of who is the real father of a young couple's child, and, in his deepest, most commanding tone of voice, Ray had said, "*Ruth*, I thought we had agreed never to discuss the paternity of that goddamn kid!" Mary and the director and the other actors had cracked up laughing and Mary, sniffling and giggling, had replied in a half-suppressed giggle, "Oh yes, Doctor, I swear, never again—" And this scene they had fun with early in the morning was the one that by taping time in the afternoon would work so movingly and seriously.

We get our iced tea and Mary says, "I think a lot of people are patronizing about soap opera because they don't know what goes into it, the amount of thought and work and effort. I've worked on Broadway and I've done two films, but the demands of *this* are much more intense, for everyone involved.

"But even though that's the public's attitude, I think it's changing now. The attitude toward it is changing among professional theater people. There used to be scorn for it, when there was a lot of theater work available. Now many of the best actors are working in soaps, or want to work in them. Most theater people I talk to are very respectful of what I'm doing now."

I wonder how she feels about the story itself, about the standard clichés of soap opera being unreal, a frothy fantasy.

"No," she says, "I really don't feel that way. Take the scene you saw this afternoon. This was a deeply understandable situation between two people who are both married for the second time and trying hard to make it work, but they are having this conflict over one of their children. Well, people *do* get into conflicts over their children, marriage *is* difficult, such arguments *are* painful.

"One of the other criticisms about soap operas is that it's mostly two people talking to one another, and indeed the physical restrictions of a small studio and a very limited number of sets means that you have to have a lot of straight exposition, and that is very hard for an actor to do—just stand there and talk with a camera on you. But there's a tremendous satisfaction in pulling it off. And when I say it's 'restriction' I mean in terms of theater, but in terms of 'real life' the fact is you do sit around a lot and simply make conversation."

As we are doing now. We finish our iced tea, still talking, and Mary says she is terribly sorry, she would like to go on talking but she has an appointment—she is going to Elizabeth

Arden for a facial, which she says is something she does "to be good to myself." I pay the iced-tea check and we are still talking as we go out to look for a cab, and Mary is telling how she doesn't mind getting her scripts only a week in advance, not knowing what is going to happen to *Ruth Martin* in the story.

"I enjoy playing it as it is, one day at a time—that's how life is, you don't know what's going to happen tomorrow either."

I wave a cab over for her, and as I open the door Mary pauses and says, "You know, for instance, I'm getting into this cab, and you're going to get another cab, and one of them might crash or something, we don't know what will happen to us, even today, much less tomorrow or a week from now."

I agree, and Mary gets in the cab, thanking me for the iced tea.

And I thank Mary. And hope to God nothing happens to her cab. Any of her cabs.

The rehearsal room of the "All My Children" show bears a basic spiritual resemblance to the waiting lounge of the Cedar Rapids, Iowa, airport. Except it doesn't even have any windows. There are gray, blank walls whose only decoration is a bulletin board with assorted announcements, messages, and notices of interest to the cast. There are some filing cabinets and storage boxes, folding chairs, a large wooden cabinet with many pigeonholes labeled with the names of the cast where their fan mail is stuffed, a coffee machine, and one long anonymous sort of table where the actors sit around in the morning waiting to do their first rehearsals. There is a box of doughnuts on the table, and the members of the day's cast munch the doughnuts, sip coffee from styrofoam cups, read their scripts or the New York *Times* or books they have brought, while they wait for the director to call them for their scenes. On this particular day Eileen Letchworth, perhaps feeling especially dramatic after her successful full-face appearance as *Margo* with her new face lift, is reading a book on Eleanora Duse, and Ray MacDonnell has brought along a book on poverty in America by the sociologist Richard Cloward.

It is eight o'clock in the morning. I am reminded of the great Columbia professor of English, and poet, Mark Van Doren, who said to my class, in sympathy after we had taken our final exams in a huge anonymous hall, "I think it is a wonder that you gentlemen are able to write anything at all in such a *godforsaken* place."

In the same vein I wonder how these actors are able to begin their creation of a drama that by midafternoon will be taped for a nationwide audience. One of the ways they do it is, they play. They ham it up, twisting lines, improvising jokes, breaking into thick, incongruous dialects, and bantering back and forth among themselves and the director. Sometimes Ray MacDonnell, reading some heavy bit of dialogue for his role as the stolid *Dr. Joe Martin, sings* his lines. Like "Oh, *Ruth,* my dear, I think we are facing a serious cri-sis!" Done operatically, with flourish. It's a way of getting through the day—a day that eventually will include at least five rehearsals and a final taping, and God knows how many informal practice sessions with two actors in the same scene "running their lines" to make sure they're getting them completely memorized.

Right now director Henry Kaplan is out in the middle of the floor, holding a script, going through a scene with Judy Barcroft and Peter White, who play the roles of *Anne Tyler* and her brother *Lincoln,* the grown children of the most prestigious family in all of Pine Valley. *Anne* is a beautiful and appealing blond woman who is recently divorced and living at home and doing volunteer work at the Pine Valley Hospital, and her brother *Lincoln* is a handsome and successful young lawyer. *Anne* and *Linc* are very sympathetic to one another's problems, which often center on their socialite mother *Phoebe.* They are a close brother and sister, very mutually supportive. But that is all in the show. Right now they are actors Judy Barcroft and Peter White, rehearsing a scene at eight in the morning. Judy, who will later be the lovely *Anne* in an appropriately chic outfit, is wearing a sweater and jeans and dark glasses and has a scarf over her head, and Peter, who will later be the well-turned-out *Lincoln Tyler* in a spiffy suit, is now wearing jeans and a sweater and loafers and a well-worn old sports jacket. At this point most of the cast are dressed in this manner, the women with their hair in curlers, the men with comfortable old jackets and jeans or corduroy pants and loafers or sneakers.

Judy and Peter have just run through their scene once and before going through it again Judy turns to Henry Kaplan and, pointing to Peter, says, "I want to ask you a few things about this man."

"Shoot," says Henry, knowing what's coming—not in fact but in essence.

"Does he dye his hair?"

"I'll bite, does he?" Henry asks obligingly.

"No," says Judy, "it's prematurely orange."

"Now ask me if he's a model," Judy says.

"O.K., is he a model?"

"No—he's full-scale!"

There are giggles and moans from the actors at the table chewing their doughnuts.

"O.K.," Henry says. "Now that we've got that cleared up, let's take it from the top."

In this scene *Anne* will be sitting in the Tyler living room when *Lincoln* comes home from work. *Lincoln* asks if she's had a good day and *Anne* says yes, no one was home and she really enjoyed being alone in the house—she read a book, she wrote some letters. *Anne* has just returned home from Seattle, where she had gone to stay with her brother *Linc* and recuperate from her painful divorce, and she is enjoying being back in Pine Valley and living in the family home again. When Judy comes to the part about how she spent the day reading a book and writing letters, she looks up from her script and asks, "Who could I write any letters to? I don't have any friends."

Henry looks up from his own script and says, "Maybe you made some friends in Seattle."

"I doubt it," she says.

Later in this scene there is a reference to *Amy Tyler*, who hasn't been on the show since its beginning, when actress Rosemary Prinz played the part, and Peter White, who has only been on a year or so, asks Henry, "*Amy Tyler?* Who is this *Amy Tyler?*"

"She's your ex-wife—from a long time ago," Henry explains. "*Amy Tyler*—she was Rosemary Prinz."

Peter says, "Really? Rosemary Prinz? She was my sister in 'The Secret Storm.'"

Henry says, "Well, now she's your ex-wife and she's off in Switzerland or something doing good works."

"That's funny," Judy says. "Rosemary Prinz off in Switzerland? I just saw her last week at a cocktail party."

"So Rosemary's my ex-wife now?" Peter says. "And used to be my sister. It's a small world."

"It sure is," Judy says. "In this business, anyway."

Judy goes back to the script, clears her throat, and reads a line about how her former husband, *Nick Davis,* has just opened a restaurant in Pine Valley, and she says she hopes he succeeds but it seems an awfully bad time to be opening a restaurant, what with prices the way they are.

"Yeah," says Henry. "We're very big on inflation this week."

At the lunch break I join Bud and Henry Kaplan at McGlade's, and they ask me how I'm doing and I say I'm being impressed by what the actors have to do and go through for a daily program. They nod in agreement and Henry says:

"Not everyone can do it. We've had very good Broadway actors fall apart here, because they're not used to doing things in such a short concentrated time. Some of them just can't memorize lines that fast, whole new scripts day after day. I was at a party in Connecticut recently and a very experienced Broadway actress got to talking with me and she said she once tried doing a soap but she couldn't do it. She said she had never been so scared, not on any stage, trying to memorize the lines and the stage directions."

Back in the studio I find Stephanie Braxton sitting in the control room waiting for her scene in the run-through after lunch. This is the first time the entire program is rehearsed in sequence, for lines, timing, and positioning, putting the elements all together before the next rehearsal, which is the dress. Stephanie has just come from makeup, where she had been under the dryer, and her long black hair is up in curlers. She is wearing a blue print blouse and a short green skirt and espadrilles, and she is sitting in one of the brown swivel chairs, one foot tucked up beneath her, the other tapping the floor with what seems to be a little impatience.

She tells me this is her third soap, she had been on "Love Is a Many-Splendored Thing" and "The Secret Storm." On "The Secret Storm" she had played Laura, who was something like the *Tara* she plays now, but "Laura was more passive, more frightened."

I ask if before she played *Tara* she had watched Karen Gorney, the original actress who played the part, and she says, "I think I only caught her once, very briefly. Everything was happening so quickly on 'Secret Storm,' before it went off the air, and there wasn't much time. Besides, I don't think it matters much, trying to copy the person who played the role before you. On a soap, they're hiring you for your *aura*. They don't want you to study so you can learn to be like someone different.

"I don't mean you don't work on the part. But you do it your own way. You work, and it can be very interesting work for an actress. It keeps the juices flowing. You even do things you're quite pleased with. But I think a great deal more could be done if there weren't such restrictions due to budget. I'd like to see us have more location work, more flexibility in sets and production. I think there's a lot of talent on soaps better than what you have on nighttime, but the nighttime shows *look* better because of the locations and the production facilities.

"The scripts we get here vary widely—some are right on, they're so natural and right you can learn them in five minutes. But in general I wish we could have more silences, less obvious lines—less having to *say* 'I love you,' or 'I hate you' or 'I'm scared,' as if the audience were deaf and dumb and blind.

What I like about 'The Waltons' is there's a whole lot conveyed without the people saying anything."

I mention that I've heard a lot of the cast members here are
friends with one another, and I wonder if she socializes with
any of them.

"No," she says. "I come here and do my job, and when I'm
through I want to go home and relax and forget about it."

She has to go back to makeup now and have her hair
combed out.

After the run-through following lunch, Henry comes in
from the set and seats himself behind the console, to watch
the dress rehearsal on one of the monitors. It is now that
Henry picks up his baton. Henry has a baton. He uses it like
an orchestra director, raising it and lowering it as scenes
begin and move, as he says, "Follow her, follow her in,
thaaat's it. . . . Cue *Mona* and—*take one*. . . . Music . . .
tight-en that shot, O.K., pull back now, loooooosen . . . yes,
good. . . ."

During the taping the baton is almost constantly in action,
though none of the actors can see it, nor cameramen or crew;
it is not for them, it is for Henry, and I have no doubt it helps,
gives him a sense of specific and tangible control over the
movement, the action. By the time the actual tape is done the
baton seems to me more like a wand, and Henry who wields it
the magician who has cast this spell, this half-hour self-contained but continuing story, this *world* and its inhabitants that
ten million people follow, transfixed, believing. After all the
intricate and tedious and arduous work of the day, when the
theme music swells at the end and the crawl with the names
of all those people who have made it happen moves up the
screen, I can understand why Kay Campbell cries. If you have
been there since eight o'clock that morning you can feel,
along with the cast, the sense of exhaustion, and accom-
plishment, the whole thing done in one day against considerable odds, against the clock, against the innumerable unexpected problems, the stuck doors and protruding branches,
the technical breakdowns and human failings. Against all that

it works, it happens, it is made, and it seems as though you have witnessed a kind of minor miracle.

Out in the hall I run into Kay Campbell, ebullient, and she asks how I'm liking it and I say I'm hopelessly hooked on the whole thing.

Kay laughs and says, "Isn't it fun? All of *us* are hooked on it, too. We can't wait to find out what happens next!"

What happens next in my own story is I decide to interview the show's two principal heavies.

The debonair and wily cad *Nick Davis*.

And the beautiful, conniving super-bitch *Erica Kane*.

Bud looks at his master sheet that shows which actors will be on the set which days, and finds a time when I can catch both Larry Keith and Susan Lucci.

I come in about quarter after nine that day and go up to the second-floor rehearsal room. The coffee and doughnuts are gone by this time, and so are Larry and Susan, but I figure I have plenty of time to get hold of them later during the day, and I sit down to listen to a scene between *Margo* and her attractive young assistant in the Boutique, *Kitty Shea*. I have admired *Kitty*, who during the past year has emerged from being a depressed and wishy-washy little thing letting *Nick Davis* trample all over her, to an alert, more confident and positive young woman improving herself by taking night courses in business and culture. It occurs to me I might also then have reason to admire the actress who has so convincingly portrayed this transformation, Francesca James. Francesca and Eileen, as *Kitty* and *Margo*, are sitting opposite one another on folding chairs, running their lines, leaving the scripts on their laps and only consulting them if they forget something.

Kitty: "Well, *Margo*, I think those two people have a definite *antipathy* toward one another."

Margo (clasping a hand to a breast, her eyes wide in mock astonishment): "They have a definite—what did you say?—a definite *what?*"

Kitty (grinning, mouthing each syllable as she leans toward *Margo*): "A definite *an-tip-a-thy*. That's what."

Margo (hamming it up even more): "An-*tip*-a-thy! Well now! And where did we learn a word like that?"

Kitty (with put-on smugness): "At my night school business course, that's where!" (She sticks out her tongue.)

Margo: "Well, I do declare!"

They both start laughing and production assistant Sherrell Hoffman presses her stopwatch and tells them O.K., they can go now. I introduce myself to Francesca and ask if she has a few minutes to talk before going to the set. She says sure, she has to stop off in her dressing room anyway and we can talk there till she gets called on the loudspeaker.

I realize my objective this day is to talk with Susan and Larry, but I justify talking to Francesca not only because I wanted to do that anyway sometime and now is convenient, but also because I know she once played an *Erica*-type bitch on another soap and perhaps she can give me some insights about it before my interview with Susan.

On Francesca's dressing table are copies of *A History of Egypt* and *The Ides of March* by Thornton Wilder, and she explains that in addition to doing "All My Children" she is currently commuting once a week to St. Louis, where she is playing Cleopatra in Shaw's *Caesar and Cleopatra* at the Loretto-Hilton repertory theater.

She has been on Broadway in *The Rothschilds* and she has also been on several soaps before this, the last one "the show next door," "One Life to Live," where she played the part of a really evil villainess named Marcy Wade.

"I turned into a psychotic murderer—I got so nasty that they had to kill me off."

I ask if that sort of role is more draining than others and Francesca says, "No, in fact being a straight-out villainess is the easiest—you instigate things, and so you're the center of things, the magnet, and the action takes place around you."

I ask if it's depressing playing a role like that, if it affects your personal life.

"Not the villainess thing, no, it's so black-and-white and

1. Agnes Nixon, "the creator," at home preparing the further fates of the citizens of Pine Valley.

2. Lawrence Keith, whose acting turned the originally doomed villain *Nick Davis* into a more likable and thus less expendable character.

3. Susan Lucci, looking petulant and beautiful as usual in her role as *Erica*, the fans' favorite femme fatale.

4. Director Henry Kaplan with his faithful baton, "orchestrating" the day's episode from the control room; at his side with a stop watch is assistant director Sherrell Hoffman.

5. One of the four small sets that are the daily allotment for the drama, with cameraman Frank Venta in position to shoot a scene between star-crossed lovers *Tara* (Stephanie Braxton) and *Phil* (Nick Benedict).

6. Fra Heflin, sister of actor Van, is being prepared for her role as the sincere and long-suffering *Mona Kane* by studio hair stylist Judi Goodman.

predictable, and it's not really close to your own life at all. But what did affect me was the role of *Kitty* the way she was until recently. You remember, when she was dating *Nick* and then married to *Nick*, she was a real loser, always depressed about something, always letting everyone take advantage of her. Playing that was a real downer. It really began to get to me personally.

"When you play a role like that you have to draw on what makes *you* feel worthless and it really begins to affect you, how you react to people in your real life. And I think that is much more true on a soap, where you're playing the same character day in and day out, but she is doing different things, getting into different situations. In a play you do the same lines all the time, and you can put it out of your head when you leave the theater. But on a daily serial, you're memorizing new lines, playing new scenes all the time, but all based on this loser personality, and it really gets to you.

"I went to Agnes and told her how it was affecting me and asked if she couldn't do something a little more upbeat with *Kitty* and she did. She had *Kitty* start seeing a therapist, and getting a new job and an apartment of her own, and begin to have pride in herself. It really made a difference to me personally, it really got me out of what I felt I was falling into emotionally."

So the old *Kitty* was transformed into the new *Kitty* because Francesca was getting too depressed playing the old *Kitty* and now is much happier with her new—I mean with *Kitty's* new—personality.

She says, however, that the villainess roles are the ones the audience seems most interested in.

"Everyone is always asking me about Susan Lucci. Whenever I meet someone who watches the show the first thing they want to know is, 'Is she really like that? Is she really such a bitch?'"

"And?" I ask.

Francesca smiles, seeing, I think, that I might be such a questioner and shakes her head slowly and emphatically.

"No, no, Susan is marvelous, and she's wonderful to work

with. We had a scene last week where *Erica* was going to New York to have an abortion and *Erica* and *Kitty* kept saying goodbye. I mean, in the script we had to say goodbye about sixteen times, and in rehearsal when we did the last goodbye we both broke out laughing. And we realized that was real—that if in real life you found yourself having to keep saying goodbye to a friend, after a while you'd both see it was funny, so we did it that way on the show, and someone from another show who saw it called our director and said the scene was terrific and wondered if it had been written in or if it just happened.

"There's a lot of that on this show—people really work with each other, help each other. This and 'One Life' are the two nicest shows I've ever been on. And they're not all like that. I was on one where the tension was so great it was unbelievable —everyone was afraid of making a mistake. That kind of atmosphere makes everything impossible. As a result, nothing creative was happening. The first rule of acting is relaxation, and we have that here. On this show, people really listen to each other."

The loudspeaker is calling for *Kitty Shea* now, and Francesca excuses herself and stands up and I walk down the hall with her and ask if that scene I'd watched her and Eileen rehearse about "antipathy" was a put-on, an improvisation they were doing, and she grinned and said, "Oh no—I mean, it was all in the script, we were just fooling around with it."

By the time of the taping the same lines were done straight, convincingly, with just enough edge of a put-on remaining to make it seem like just the way two friends would discuss the matter.

I go onto the set, careful to step over the snake-sized camera cords as they move, and in general stay out of the way. Henry Kaplan is moving *Erica* to a better position for the camera and she smiles and says, "Careful now, I'm very delicate now, remember?"

Both *Erica* and Susan are pregnant.

Over on the set of the Château Nick Davis, *Nick* is taking *Lincoln* to see the place, and introduces him to *Freddie*, the

headwaiter. This is just the rehearsal for blocking and mark-
ing, and so it's still O.K. to kid around with lines and *Nick* is
saying, "*Freddie,* I want you to meet *Linc*—he's the *missing
Linc, Freddie!*"

Linc pays no attention, looks around him, and says, "Pretty
fair place you've got here, *Nick.*"

"That's an understatement," *Nick* says aggressively. "You
know, I took a big hand in designing this place. I hope
[chuckle] I didn't make too many mistakes."

Linc takes another look of cool appraisal and says, "From
what I can see, *Nick,* you really goofed."

When they finish their improvised lines, Larry goes to the
piano and points with distaste to a candelabrum.

He looks around at the stage manager and says, "What's all
this Liberace stuff?"

By the next rehearsal the candelabrum is gone.

I am able to catch Larry Keith before the run-through, and
we sit in his dressing room and talk about playing villains.
Affixed to his mirror is a picture of a giraffe bending down to
take a drink of water and under it are the words: "There must
be a better way."

"Before this I was on 'Another World,'" Larry says. "And
the guy I played on that was an out-and-out villain. This guy
I play now was supposed to be, but I didn't want to make him
that black-and-white. Actors, you see, can help shape the role
—they can play *against* the material, the way they move, the
way they speak, their expressions—that can change the feeling
of a character. That's what I did with *Nick Davis.*"

Aside from whatever dramatic reasons Larry may have had
for wanting to save *Nick* from out-and-out villainy there was a
more compelling practical reason.

"In doing this I added considerably to *Nick's* longevity. A
total villain is going to be pursued and punished, he's going to
be killed off. A more complicated character is going to have a
better chance of staying on."

So at the same time Larry was saving *Nick Davis* from an
untimely death he was saving Larry his job.

Larry knows his character inside out, and explains some of

the background to me: "This character, *Nick Davis,* was originally from Pine Valley but he got a girl pregnant and ran
away from home and joined the Navy. The child was adopted
by the sister of the natural mother. *Nick* fled from all this responsibility, knocked around a lot, got to be a bit of a con
man, became sophisticated and suave in a very—*earthy*—kind
of way. But he couldn't shake off his roots, had to 'make it'
back home, had to come back and prove himself. *Nick* never
went far in school, he grew up with a gutter fighter's instinct
for survival. He always wants to be approved of by others, he
wants to upgrade himself."

In fact Larry has upgraded *Nick's* position in Pine Valley
by suggesting to Agnes a year or so ago a new job for him.

"*Nick* used to be a dancing instructor, he opened a dance
studio in Pine Valley," Larry explains. "Well, at some cast
party I said to Agnes, 'Listen, this dancing school stuff is for
the birds. Why don't you have someone die and leave *Nick* a
lot of money so he can open up a really nice restaurant-
nightclub?'"

Agnes said she'd think about it.

Besides upgrading *Nick's* social status from dance instructor
to nightclub owner, Larry's suggestion would have still another positive effect on the wily *Nick's* career. If a man owns
his own nightclub, and he can sing, why it follows that he can
sing in his nightclub.

And it so happens Larry Keith can sing.

In fact he started out as a singer and he says, "That's what
I like best. I helped work my way through college singing
club dates, had my own act, worked for four years. My first
professional theater job was as a chorus singer in *My Fair
Lady.* I also sang at churches and synagogues, went to Brooklyn College and the Indiana University School of Music. I also
understudied Alfred Drake in *Kismet.* I said to Agnes, why
not let *Nick* sing a little on the show? If he had that nightclub, he could do it."

Agnes thought about that, too.

"Well, a few months later, Agnes was at our annual Christmas party, and she came up to me and said, 'I have a surprise

for you.' I said, 'What's that?' And Agnes said, '*Nick's* going to get his nightclub!'"

And of course, once he got his own nightclub, he got to sing.

One of *Nick's* trademarks on the show is his clothes, which are much flashier and more daring than those that any of the other Pine Valley men wear. *Nick* tends to go for wide, zooming lapels that give a Satan-like effect, suits with belted jackets and numerous buckles and buttons, suede shoes, and wide, colorful ties. These outfits are part of *Nick's* personality, and I ask Larry if the costume designer specially picks these clothes to fit the *persona* of *Nick Davis*.

"Those are all my own clothes," Larry says proudly.

"Oh," I say.

"I'm the only actor in the show," he explains, "who does this—who wears his own clothes in the part. I feel *Nick* should be dressed a little—well, not exactly mod, but stylishly. You see, he's so insecure he has to show he has fine taste."

"Ah, I see."

Later I hear a story about how one day Larry showed up on the set wearing what one production staff member thought looked like a cross between a double-breasted jacket and a Batman cape. The production person said, "For God's sake, tell Larry Keith to take that thing off. Not even *Nick Davis* would wear a getup like *that*." But someone else explained: "Maybe *Nick Davis* wouldn't wear it, but Larry Keith would. That's his own outfit." No one told Larry that not even *Nick Davis* would wear that sort of thing.

It's time for Larry to go on the set and as I walk down the hall with him he says, "One amazing thing about acting on soaps—the recognition factor is incredible."

I ask if people recognize him as *Nick Davis* everywhere he goes.

"Well, not *every*where," Larry says. "But lots of places. On airplanes, for instance."

He stops at the door, and says, "I've rarely been on a flight where stewardesses didn't know who I was."

Nick—I mean Larry—is grinning slyly.

On the set, the stage manager is saying to a distinguished-looking gray-haired black pianist on the set of the Château Nick Davis, "As the scene opens, you should just be kind of twinkling, in the background."

"*Twinkling?*" the pianist asks.

"Maybe he means your eyes," a cameraman says.

I go back to the console, where Henry and Bud are watching a close-up of *Erica* on the monitor.

"I don't like *Erica's* hair," Henry tells Bud. "Let's get the hairdresser."

"*Erica* does her own hair," Bud says. "Nobody else touches her hair."

"O.K., but we ought to have the hairdresser on the set anyway."

Someone says the hairdresser is now doing *Nick's* hair.

Henry sighs. "Let me talk to *Erica*," he says.

I will soon be talking to *Erica* myself, and I am getting very nervous. I tell myself how silly that is. I remember discussing with Bud the actors and the roles they play and him telling me that "sometimes the real personality of the actor and the character come very close, but with a twist," and then quickly adding, "but Susan Lucci, who plays *Erica*, is really a lovely gal, a very sweet person. She's the one who gets the most hostility when people recognize her on the street. I don't mean they do anything but they say things to her like 'Why do you treat *Jeff* so badly?' Susan does a wine commercial in which she starts out bitchy like *Erica* and then after having ·some wine becomes very sweet. But the real Susan is a genuinely nice person."

But I find myself remembering *Erica* having a tantrum, *Erica* sneering at good-hearted *Jeff*, *Erica* reducing her mother to tears, *Erica* even intimidating *Nick Davis* with her vicious tongue. . . .

Bud introduces me to *Erica*—no, no, to Susan Lucci—during a short break, and she apologizes that she doesn't have much time right now but we can at least get started and then she'll be happy to talk with me at greater length when the taping is over. She invites me to come to her dressing room so we can at least begin the discussion. She is pleasant and informal, wearing a blouse and skirt and scuffed white clogs. But when I sit down on the small straight-backed chair in her dressing room and she sits at her dressing table, her black hair cascading around her and that smile lighting her face, that deceptive smile that has caused so much trouble and heartbreak and broken homes and misery and unrequited love; when I see that face, I simply cannot see Susan Lucci. I can only see *Erica Kane*. I have been watching that face for nearly four years and I simply can't switch my reaction to it into another formulation.

I can feel myself trembling. I am trying to ask questions and at the same time tell myself I am being embarrassingly silly. My pen is making scrawly marks in my notebook, like the writing of a Neanderthal man who holds the pen with his fist.

Susan is telling me brightly how after she got out of college she landed a role in a movie and she thought she had it made and was going to be a big star just like that, but the movie was never even released and there she was looking for work again.

The words are Susan's but the voice is *Erica's*—I have heard it as *Erica's* voice for almost four years, there's no way it's going to suddenly sound like this nice, friendly Susan-person's voice.

She tells me how well she remembers the day she auditioned for "All My Children." "It was raining, and I almost didn't come." She got the job and has stayed with it ever since, and will return to it after she has her baby.

She looks at me smiling, waiting for me to ask something, but I have dropped my notebook. I have a hard time picking it up, and when I do I say I really enjoyed talking to her, and maybe we can talk some more later (even though she obviously still has more time now), and I scurry out, not looking right or left as I go straight through the hall to the doorway and outside.

I walk. I walk from Sixty-seventh Street to Seventy-second Street and back. I try to think. I think about how I have sometimes had these kinds of nervous attacks of trembling when I've been on television talk shows promoting some book or other but usually after the first few minutes the fit passes and I get along O.K. But trying to interview *Erica*, I knew the shaking was not going to stop, it was getting worse as I went along. I wonder if it's something like stage fright, something that actors experience and learn to overcome.

In a flash, I see exactly what to do. I will talk the whole thing over with nurse *Ruth Martin*. I will invite her for another iced tea at McGlade's, and I will pour out my heart to her, seeking her aid and advice. Just thinking about it, I feel better, imagining the warm and sympathetic response, the soothing comfort, and the solution to my problem. She will tell me some secret bit of lore of the stage, a technique devised in Elizabethan times and passed on through generations of thespians, a cure for nervous quaking in public. It will be some seemingly simple method, like squeezing your left earlobe and counting backward from seven, or taking a deep breath and imagining yourself floating down the Nile on a silken raft . . . *something*. I will pledge to nurse *Ruth* never to reveal this secret to anyone else, and of course it will work like a charm and I will never have that problem any more.

Then I have another flash, a kind of critical revelation of the first flash.

"You silly son of a bitch," I say to myself. "You are slipping into the show. You are thinking like you're a person who lives in Pine Valley. You are not responding to the actors who work on 'All My Children,' you are responding to the characters they portray in Pine Valley. You were scared by *Erica*, and now you want to go to nurse *Ruth* for comfort and advice. The next thing you know you'll be asking *Kitty Shea* to have a drink with you at the Château Nick Davis, or stopping by Grandma *Kate Martin's* for cookies and milk."

I remind myself I am not in Pine Valley. I am standing on West Sixty-seventh Street in New York City, outside the ABC–TV studios. It is a cool and pleasant autumn afternoon.

And I am sweating like crazy.

Act II

THE CREATOR

When the crawl listing the credits moves up the screen at the end of each "All My Children" show, to the accompaniment of its compelling theme music (recorded by an orchestra and *not* on an organ, as the cast and staff are quick to point out), the first line reads:

Created by Agnes Nixon

Not just written, you understand, but *created.* In other words, Agnes Nixon invented this whole thing, this entire little world that spins before the eyes of more than ten million viewers five days a week, fifty-two weeks a year, and, as creator, she is the principal person who keeps it spinning.

When I first meet her I say I am very impressed to be talking to the "creator," since I really am a fan.

Agnes laughs and says, "Oh, I know all about it."

"You mean from the letter I wrote you?" I ask.

"No, from Mary Fickett," Agnes says.

She winks.

I blush.

Mary must have told her about what I later think of as "the exotic iced tea" we had together, in which my enthusiasm for the show as well as for Mary/nurse *Ruth* was blatantly obvious.

Agnes says Mary told her after talking with me, "Either he's a fan, or this is the biggest con job in history!"

I begin to realize Agnes is not only the creator of the show but head of the "family," for "All My Children" is a family indeed as well as a TV soap opera. Sometimes it's hard to tell where one leaves off and the other begins.

In the family, as in any family, almost everyone knows almost everything about everyone else, and information about outsiders or visitors or newcomers is conveyed with telegraphic speed. And Agnes, as head of the family, knows the most and the soonest.

Agnes is on one of her biweekly trips to New York from Philadelphia for several days to confer with her writers and producer, and she is staying as usual at the Hotel Lombardy, the traditionally favorite hostelry of Procter and Gamble executives, and so a sort of headquarters for all the soap opera world. She takes a one-bedroom suite in order to have a living room for meetings and conferences, and we are having cocktails there with several old friends of Agnes' whom she hasn't seen in a long time. I urge her to go ahead talking with them, since we have a formally scheduled interview later in the week and I just wanted this opportunity to meet her first socially.

I realize I've had a mistaken image of Agnes, derived, I think, from her title as "creator." That sounds awesome. I have found myself in the studio wondering if any large, imposing woman I saw could be Agnes.

It couldn't.

The once-young-man-about-town-in-publishing who knew Agnes in what she calls her salad days, recalled her with a description that still applies, for she indeed is "slim, with reddish-blond hair, and a wonderful smile." If there is any difference in appearance between the Agnes of then and now it could only be that she was then an attractive young girl and she is now an attractive mature woman.

I had imagined Agnes as being formidable, and she is, but not in the way I supposed. I was thinking of a person who is formidable in an obvious way, in voice or size, and perhaps topped off with a big hat. None of that applies.

The formidable part of Agnes is her eyes. They look at you straight, and you know it would be a big mistake to try to appear before them as anything other than what you are. But it's a matter of honesty rather than intimidation. I am reminded of the unsolicited comment of Fra Heflin, who plays *Mona Kane* on "All My Children," when she told me:

"Agnes is terrific to work for. I never feel she's a 'driven career woman,' if you know what I mean. So many times you get a hard and bitter career woman in a position like hers, and she's simply not like that."

When I come to know her better, when we regard one another as friends, Agnes says in a letter that in spite of everything she still sometimes feels like the scared little girl who got on the L & N railroad in Nashville to go off to Chicago for the first time all those years ago. The sense of that is inside the charm, the talent, the perception. People who are never scared, or never remember they were, may create many kinds of things, from factories to wars to wardrobes, but they don't create good stories.

Agnes is a natural storyteller, in "real life" as well as for her serial. And she loves it, loves the telling. You can see it in her gestures and hear it in the pace and modulation of her voice, which I find especially familiar and comforting with its pleasant traces of Midwest twang and Southern drawl.

One of the stories she is telling me and her friends is interrupted by the door buzzer. Agnes gets up, starts to go to answer it, then turns to me with an expression of mock terror and says, "Maybe it's *Erica!*"

Oh God. Of course. She's heard about my flubbed-up interview with *Erica*—I mean, with Susan Lucci!

I might as well face it. She's heard about everything.

Early on a hot, gummy New York morning a few days later Agnes is telling me about the genesis of "All My Children" as we sip coffee in her living room at the Lombardy. Agnes, wearing a trim tan pants suit, has not put on any makeup yet, and she looks more pale and intense than the night she served cocktails for me and her friends. As she tells me about the origin of the program I am reminded of the time Lawrence Keith, who plays *Nick Davis*, tried to explain to some student interviewers from the Brooklyn College radio station that Agnes is "the cree-ay-tor" of the program, which means, as he put it, "this is *her baby*."

And, as Agnes talks now, it becomes clear that of all her TV "babies" this is the favorite, the special one, the "pet," maybe because among other things it had such a hard time at first, was literally lost at a crucial point in its development, and even Agnes gave up on it for a while before it was finally born.

"I worked on it at first in my spare time—well, what spare time I had while I was writing another show and taking care of the family," she explains. "It was a long gestation period, about six months. I started with *Chuck* and *Phil* and *Tara*. The two young men are best friends from boyhood, and both are in love with the same girl. It's a frequent situation, I think —anyway it struck me, you know, you have your own litmus paper for picking up such situations, your writer's antenna tells you if it's something you can work with, something you can draw on.

"Besides the young-love aspect of it, I wanted to portray the friendship between the young men. I think such friendships are so important, and can be very beautiful. I think I write a lot about friendship partly in protest against those who say everyone is so tough and you're not supposed to show emotions. Especially men.

"I also wanted to get into the generational thing, the relations of parents and children. I felt if we showed what the kids were *feeling*, maybe parents could get a different perspective. I think we have a great opportunity, through dramatic entertainment, to help explain liberals to hard-hats, for instance, and parents to children, and vice versa—to open people's minds a little bit.

"And besides the parents and children I wanted to have the

older generation, like Grandma *Kate Martin*. She's a sort of combination of my own grandmother and another Kate who was very influential in my life. I think these older people we lean and depend on are so important, they mean so much to us, the *Kate Martins* of this world."

So Agnes was creating her own new fictional world, putting the people in it, establishing the relationships, building the generations.

That Christmas of 1965 she and her family went to St. Croix, and Agnes took along what was now a rough draft of the presentation for "All My Children" and five sample scripts. She worked on the material on the beach, editing and revising, and by the time the vacation was over Agnes felt she was making real progress.

When the family got back home they found that one suitcase was missing.

It was the one that contained all the manuscript material for "All My Children." There were no carbons or copies.

When she tells this story I utter a phrase that in the coming months becomes a kind of password between us, a comment made whenever we have a seemingly incredible or melodramatic story to tell that happened to one of us or one of our friends or acquaintances in "real life":

"Talk about *soap opera!*"

A few months later, without explanation, the suitcase turned up. Agnes worked on revisions, and when she was satisfied, presented the manuscript to Procter and Gamble. They took an option on it, but later dropped it.

"I was heartbroken," Agnes says. "P & G *said* they liked it, and the official reason it didn't get on the air was that there wasn't any network time available. But I felt there must be something wrong with it. I put it out of my sight. I literally put it in a drawer. It made me doubt myself, but I'm not ashamed of that. Anyone worth his salt has a certain amount of insecurity.

"I said to myself, 'O.K., I'll just forget about that, and I'll start with a clean slate.' I was asked to take over the writing of 'Another World,' which was down at the bottom of the ratings, and within a year I brought it up to Number Two. That's really how I got to be known in the industry. Shortly after that, ABC asked me to create my own show for them. I didn't even think about 'All My Children.' I wanted to start with something completely new."

The serial she created, "One Life to Live," was not only new for Agnes, it was in many ways new in the history and tradition of soap operas.

"When I created 'One Life to Live,'" she tells me, "I achieved one of my personal ambitions, which was to take soap operas out of WASP Valley. We hired an actress who was black but very light-skinned, who could pass for white, and created a story around her. I had the actress, Ellen Holly, help and advise me in the writing. We tried to do a story that would force people to examine their own prejudices. For the first four months of the program, the viewers thought the woman was white; then we had her fall in love with a black doctor. Well, due to the advice Ellen had given me, about how blacks are sometimes prejudiced against one another due to economic and class factors and shades of skin coloration, we had the black doctor's proud and well-to-do family reject Ellen because she had been passing for white and thereby rejecting her own race.

"I also wrote in a lower-income Polish family with both parents dead and two very different brothers—one who quit high school and was a truck driver, and the one who became a doctor. The doctor fell in love with the older daughter of Victor Lord, the wealthy WASP socialite, and of course he's prejudiced against the doctor because of being Polish, and the doctor's truck-driver brother is prejudiced against the Lords because they're *not* Polish. . . ."

The program was not only soap opera's biggest melting pot, it was also a smash hit.

"I got a lot of recognition from that show," Agnes says, "and I gained a lot of confidence from its success.

"Once the show was established, the head of daytime TV for ABC came to my house and said the network wanted me to create another one. I said, 'I can't, I don't have an idea for another one.'

"After he left, my husband Bob said, 'What about "All My Children"?'

"I asked him if he really thought it was good enough. He said he did, so I got it out and read it again. Well, to tell the truth, after I read it and Bob asked me how I felt about it now, I said, 'I love it.'"

So did ABC.

And so, very soon, did millions of viewers.

Agnes is one of them.

"I rarely go to the set," she says, "even when I'm in New York. I prefer to watch the show at home. I get a different perspective and I think I'm more constructively critical by seeing it that way, like everyone else does. Watching it at home, I'm just another one of the ladies following 'my story' and eating the leftovers."

Agnes Nixon and her family live in a house in Bryn Mawr, Pennsylvania, on the Philadelphia "Main Line" that looks exactly like a home in Pine Valley described in the presentation of "All My Children" as "a rambling white house with black shutters shaded by the sweeping boughs of giant pine trees."

Inside the house, just off the kitchen, is a small, comfortable room where four rather battered and patched leather swivel chairs are arranged around a low wooden table, facing a large color television set. This is where Agnes watches "her program" every day.

With red gingham curtains at the windows and Agnes' husband Bob's mementos and pictures from his service in the Navy on the wall, the room is warm and homey, and even more so at this particular time because Agnes' two-year-old granddaughter Ceara is here for a visit and her dolls and toys are scattered around. A bright green cloth frog is perched on the windowsill, and on the floor around the tables are a Weebles airport and a Fisher-Price family barn that emits a mooing sound when its doors are opened.

Agnes and I are sitting at the wooden table having homemade vegetable soup for lunch and waiting for the program to
come on. In the background a game show is running on the
television and Ceara is playing with the toy barn, so that every
so often our talk is punctuated with authentic-sounding
"moooooos."

We are talking about how many of the fans consider the
characters in the show "real people" and write to them that
way, and Agnes says the same thing was true of the old radio
daytime serials; in fact, the listeners then were sometimes confused because one actor might play three or four different
parts on as many different programs.

"People listening to the programs could sometimes identify
the voices, but still they didn't think of the voices being the
voices of actors, but of 'real people.' One woman who lived on
a farm somewhere in the Midwest wrote to 'Ma Perkins' to
warn one of the women characters who was being wooed by a
gentleman to 'look out for that Mr. Pendleton, he's no good—
he's courting you at noon, and he's doing the same thing with
Portia [in "Portia Faces Life"] at four o'clock, *but he's
using a different name!*'"

When "All My Children" comes on we push back our soup
bowls and devote full attention to the program. Agnes points
out things I would not have noticed, like an actress gazing
away from the person she is talking to, a baffled expression in
her eyes; she forgot her line and is looking for the
TelePrompTer. At a commercial break Agnes asks if the scene
just preceding it bothered me and I say it didn't but wonder
why she asked. It was a scene in which Grandma *Kate Martin*
calls her son *Dr. Joe Martin* to ask about the condition of her
grandson *Little Phillip Tyler,* who is in the hospital with a
ruptured spleen after falling from a treehouse. People who
had not watched the show for the past few days would not
know about the accident, but this conversation explains it to
them.

"It's the hardest thing to do," Agnes says, "without making
the story boring. But it has to be done for people who tune in

and haven't been keeping up with the show. It's always hard to make this 'recapitulation' unobtrusive."

I write down "recapitulation" and say I'm glad to know the right term for that particular storytelling device.

"Oh, I don't know if that's 'the term' for it," Agnes says. "That's just what *I* call it."

In another scene *Phil Brent* appears, a nice young man who is currently afflicted with a number of woes, and I remark on how tough things are for him these days.

"Not only that," Agnes says. "He's going to lose his job."

"What? You mean a nice guy like *Phil* is going to be *fired?*"

"No, not fired, laid off," Agnes explains. "You know, he has this ecology job, with the Environmental Protection Agency."

"I know, it's one of the few things the poor guy has going for him."

"That's right, but I understand the EPA really *is* laying people off, and so many good people are losing jobs now because of the economy—well, I think we should show it happening. It won't be any big story thing, it won't cause any permanent harm to *Phil*, but it's a problem, a jolting one, and it's happening to a lot of people now."

I'm sorry to hear *Phil Brent* is losing his job, since he has his hands full already what with his wife *Erica* in a mental hospital after losing their baby. But, you can't argue with Fate—or, in this case, with Agnes.

Nor can you learn too much from her about what is going to happen next. Emboldened by learning that *Phil* will lose his job, I ask Agnes if *Little Phillip* is going to recover all right from his operation, but she holds up a finger and says, "I can't tell you too much, or you won't keep watching!"

After lunch we go sit in the glassed-in sun porch of Agnes' house, where winter light streams in over plants and books. Agnes draws a volume from one of the bookcases and brings it over to show me.

The volume looks familiar. It is just like the family album that appears every day as the "trademark," or, as it is professionally known, the "Bill Board" of her program. When the picture of it appears the familiar theme music begins to play, a slender hand takes a corner of the volume's cover, and slowly turns it over to the frontispiece, with the scrolled words "All My Children," decorated with an old-fashioned pink and blue flower design.

Agnes' hand turns open the cover of the album I am now holding. Instead of the title and the flower design, there are snapshots of Agnes as a little girl, with her mother and her Grandma Kate and her aunts. She lived, as James Agee put it in a reverie of a similar time and place, "disguised as a child," in Nashville, Tennessee.

There is no theme music now, as this album opens, only the pine-enclosed quiet of the porch as Agnes begins to talk of those days, those people.

The presiding, dramatic and dominant figures of her childhood seem to be her grandmother and her great-grandmother, both named Kate. Agnes has a sampler on the wall of her study signed by her grandmother, "Katie Ryan, May 17, 1875."

As a child Agnes heard the romantic tale of her great-grandmother Kate's eloping. This was in Ireland, and Katie's parents didn't approve of the young man she loved and who loved her in return, that young man named Michael Ryan.

"I don't know why the family didn't approve of him," Agnes says. "Probably because they had half an acre more than the boy's family had. That's the way it often happened in those days." But the young Katie Quinlan was not to be denied her love. Unbeknown to her family she met him at a secret spot on the moors and Michael Ryan came riding along on horseback and swooped her up and carried her off to Dublin and they sailed for America. "And she never saw her family again. She never looked back."

In the New World, in Nashville, Tennessee, Kate Ryan, daughter of Kate Quinlan, now herself married and called Kate Dalton, bore twelve children in the space of twenty-four years. One of the girls was Agnes' mother, who married a Dutchman named Eckhardt, and Kate Ryan Dalton didn't approve of him. Mr. Eckhardt and his new wife moved to Chicago, but three months after their daughter was born the mother and child returned to Nashville.

The Depression was on and her mother got a job and Agnes was mainly raised by her many aunts and Grandma Kate in a devout Catholic household.

I wonder aloud if the household was the sort that had many books, if reading and literature were a part of her growing up.

"Books? Oh yes," Agnes says, "there were books around all right. At Sunday dinner in the dining room I sat on *The Lives of the Saints* and *The Glories of the Catholic Church,* so I could reach the table."

She laughs and says, "Really, though, aside from those, my mother brought home books from the library, and *Reader's Digest* was always there, but that was pretty much it."

That is, in terms of books that was pretty much it, but that wasn't the end of sources of stories, and Agnes' favorite continuing stories were "Little Orphan Annie," "Tillie the Toiler," and "Etta Kett."

Agnes didn't just *read* these stories in the funny papers. She cut out the pictures of the characters, not just one or two pictures of each character, but pictures of each one in as many different poses as possible. (Except she didn't cut out "Little Orphan Annie" because the characters had no eyes.)

"I had pictures of all of them standing, and sitting down, and walking, and I kept them all pressed in a heavy book, so I could take them out and make up stories with them. I'd lay them out on the table, and have them talking and so on, and when I wanted one to 'sit down' I'd take out a picture of him sitting, and so on. . . .

"When I was about ten years old I gave up 'Little Orphan Annie' for Lent. But never again! It was easier to give up chocolates, or ice cream and cake."

Agnes' passion for stories at that time led to an interest in acting them. She took private lessons from a drama teacher who also was the organist at the Catholic church her family attended.

"In Nashville there were three Catholic girls' schools and

one Catholic boys' school—there were so few Catholics in the
state that all of Tennessee was only one diocese—but our
teachers and parents insulated us against anti-Catholic prejudice.

"There was a drama department at Father Ryan High
School, and from sophomore year on I was in their plays."

So Agnes went to St. Mary's College at South Bend, Indiana
and then transferred to Northwestern as a drama student, still
aspiring to act in stories rather than to write them. . . .

This is a turning point of course, the young girl going away,
but before she goes, I ask Agnes if the Grandma Kate who
seems to have presided over these years is the model of the
Grandma *Kate* in "All My Children." I say it seems odd because that *Kate* is such a warm and giving and sympathetic
personality, and I wasn't sure I got the impression her own
Grandma Kate in Nashville had been like that.

"Oh no," Agnes says, and stands up, beginning to pace
around the silver-lit sun porch. "*My* Grandma Kate carried a
heavy cane, and her word was law, and she marched around
like this"—now Agnes is making a heavy tread on the porch,
her head bowed, and pounding an imaginary cane into the
floor as she steps, saying, cheeks puffed out—"boom, boom,
boom, boom!"

Then she smiles, and sits down, dispensing with the imaginary cane, and says, "There was another Kate, too, the mother
of my best friend in college, who is still a best friend. That's
the Kate who introduced me to my husband. I guess Grandma
Kate on the program is kind of a combination of the best of
both of them—the strength and the understanding."

There is still the actress in Agnes, the imitator of Grandma
Kate in physical stance and movement as well as in intonation
and accent, and I am curious about how she turned from her
dream of performing in stories to writing them.

I know the stock answer, but now knowing Agnes a little
better, I begin to question it.

Agnes has a kind of set piece for the inevitable question of
how she happened to turn from acting to writing, and she tells
it to students and interviewers and colleagues, and everyone

enjoys it because it is impressive and "true"—you can check out the facts—and she tells it with her personal flair and sense of timing, so it is not only credible but memorable.

It goes like this:

"I was in the Drama Department at Northwestern, and in the same class with me there were Cloris Leachman, Patricia Neal, Charlton Heston, and Martha Hyer. *Well.* It was then I decided *I'd* better be a *writer!*"

As neat as this is, I find it hard to imagine Agnes running from a challenge or bowing out of a race because of stiff competition. Now, in the quiet of her sun porch and in the spirit and mood of her album's personal history, I ask if that story is all there is to it, if maybe there is more to her becoming a writer than the presence of all those talented actors.

She thinks about this, nods, and says:

"I believe it takes more than talent to be an actress. It takes —something else, something that I don't have. I'm really too much an introvert. When you're an actress, you *are* the product. I couldn't be objective about myself in those circumstances. But on paper, even though what you write may be very personal, you're a little more divorced from it, you have some distance between yourself and your work.

"But drama training certainly helped me as a writer. I had the most marvelous drama teacher, Alvina Kraus—for years she *made* the Drama Department at Northwestern. She was a disciple of Stanislavsky, and she made us really work our way into a part. I had to play a fifty-five-year-old Irish spinster and Alvina made me research that part until I knew everything about what such a woman's life would be like at that time and place in history, and then she quizzed me on it, on everything. That was wonderful training."

But Agnes' turn toward writing was not just a rejection of acting, a taking up of a second-best kind of creative work. The girl who cut out the cartoon figures and laid them out on the table to create new adventures for them was surely a natural storyteller, but the instinct for writing as writing didn't come to life until she was at Northwestern, in classes taught by a man named Lew Sarette.

It was in his classes, in creative writing and "prosody," that the spark was set, the magic thing happened.

It was then and there, Agnes recalls, that "I fell in love with *the word*. I began to love writing. Not just the story—I had always loved the story—but I began to love the words, the rhythm, the sound, the speech."

This is when one album opens to another.

The afternoon is late, and the album in my lap, the one of Agnes' early life, is heavy now. We close it.

There is no "theme music," but Agnes' granddaughter is calling for her. That will do.

Early that evening I am in the Nixons' living room and Bob Nixon and I are discussing the coming departure from the program of two attractive young people, Charlie Frank and Susan Blanchard, who play *Dr. Jeff Martin* and nurse *Mary Kennicott Martin*. In the story *Jeff* and *Mary* met at the Pine Valley Hospital and fell in love, and at the same time in "real life" Charlie and Susan met on the set of the Pine Valley Hospital in the "All My Children" studio and fell in love. Charlie has been offered a good part on a pilot for a TV series, and he has decided to leave "All My Children" and go to Hollywood to try to make it in nighttime television and then hopefully the movies. Susan, who has already had to turn down a movie role because its timing conflicted with the obligation of her "All My Children" contract, has decided to move to the Coast with Charlie, not only so she can stay with the man she loves but also so she can try her own luck as an actress out there.

"It's hard for the show," Bob says, "but I really do think it's good that young people like that have a chance to go on, to progress. And Charlie has been very fair to Ag. They both have. They wrote a very appreciative letter about their experience on the show, and they gave her plenty of advance notice."

Bob tells me how Charlie has developed tremendously as an actor, that on the original auditions the producer and casting director weren't all that interested in him.

"But Ag took the tapes of his audition home and studied them, and she still liked him. She felt he looked like her conception of *Jeff*, and that's very important. The main objection the others had was about his voice; they felt it was too nasal and didn't project well. But Ag thought he was right for the part in all other respects, so our production company paid for him to take voice lessons for three months, and then we put him on the show.

"So I'm happy for Charlie getting his chance in Hollywood now, but when anyone leaves, Ag is under a lot of pressure, having to develop a whole new story line. There's just no way around that."

He pauses and says, "Sometimes I think running this whole thing is in many ways like operating a pro football team—some players get injured, some play out their option, and new team strategy has to be designed around new people. And all the time all this is going on, you have to worry about the competition every week."

Bob Nixon knows all about this not only from observing on the sidelines as husband of the "coach," but also from his own experience in a post akin to "general manager" of a pro football team. When Agnes was asked by ABC in 1967 to package her own show, "One Life to Live," she told me, "It was inevitable then that Bob would become involved. I knew how to keep a cast budget, but I had no idea about all the other financial factors involved."

Before that Bob had been regional director of the Chrysler Corporation for the state of Pennsylvania, and in 1962 he had left that position and bought a dealership and gotten into automobile fleet leasing. When he and Agnes formed their production company, Creative Horizons, Inc., Bob became president of the company, sold his car dealership, but retained the fleet-leasing company, which he still operates.

Bob Nixon gives me the impression of being a shy and gentle man, by which I don't mean weak or vacillating, but rather that he's not going to throw his weight around for the sake of doing so, especially if doing so would hurt anyone. He is very aware of other people's feelings and reactions, and I have the sense that he is taking everything in and sorting it out and the information is going precisely in the right places for the most constructive uses. He is the sort of man who, after you get to know him a little, you feel you could trust to carry out the most delicate mission in exactly the way you'd most want it handled.

After Bob knows you a little while, you begin to discover and appreciate his wry sense of humor. I can picture him when someone later tells about Bob and Agnes being at a party where a rather blustery man came up to Bob and said, "Ah, you're Aggie's husband." Bob said that was true, and the man said he knew Aggie when she was a young girl fresh in New York writing for television, and he "revealed" to Bob that Aggie was always "a clean girl, in a dirty business!" And Bob Nixon, who has been happily married to Agnes for more than twenty years, said to his informant with a sense of mock relief, "Sir, I want you to know that after all these years, you have lifted a great burden from my mind!"

I tell Bob that despite the upcoming loss for the program of Charlie and Susan, I am happy that Ruth Warrick has returned in the role of the snippety socialite of Pine Valley, *Phoebe Tyler.* Miss Warrick is a superb actress who played the part of Charles Kane's innocent first wife in *Citizen Kane,* and has worked in movies and on Broadway as well as in several soap operas. Miss Warrick had taken off three months from "All My Children" to play in a national company of the musical *Irene,* during which time Agnes had accounted for her absence from Pine Valley by sending *Phoebe Tyler* on a "round-the-world cruise." Ruth has recently returned from her part in *Irene* and, simultaneously, *Phoebe* has returned from her "round-the-world cruise," wreaking emotional havoc on her family, friends, and foes in Pine Valley. Her reappearance has been like the unleashing of a cyclone, and I say to Bob I feel as if the pace and drama of the whole show has been accelerated by it.

"There's no doubt," Bob says, smiling, "that *Phoebe* has really"—he pauses, and lifts his hands—"has really picked things up."

Just as we are speaking of this Agnes comes in the room, smiling, holding up an envelope.

"Wait'll you see this," she says. "It came in the mail today."

Agnes takes a printed card from the envelope and hands it to me while, at the same time, she explains to Bob as I am reading it, "An invitation to Ruth Warrick's wedding. It's her fifth marriage. She's marrying 'a Cushing, from Boston,' and the wedding will be in Greenwich, Connecticut. This I can't miss. This will be marvelous."

Bob looks just a little bit worried and he asks the most practical if not the most sentimental question about the whole thing.

"Is she going on a honeymoon?"

If Ruth asks for time off for a honeymoon it will mean writing her out of the show again just when she's returned and much of the action is revolving around *Phoebe*.

Agnes sits down.

"Oh my. I *hope* not."

There is a painful silence and then Agnes shakes her head and says, "No, no, when she told me about the engagement she *promised* that if she got married she wouldn't ask for any time off. After all the time she was gone on tour with *Irene*— no. Ruth just wouldn't do that."

Agnes stands up and asks if I'd like a drink. She and Bob are going to have their usual, a blond Lillet on the rocks with an orange peel, and I say I'll try it. She brings the drinks on a tray, and I find the mild apéritif very pleasant. A few sips help to cheer us out of a kind of general brooding over the possible complications that would arise if Ruth took a honeymoon, and Agnes wisely changes the subject to the problems of *other* dramatic serials. She asks me what I think of the second and most recent series of "Upstairs, Downstairs," the highly praised British television serial that has made such a hit in America. I say I've been disappointed, I haven't enjoyed it nearly as much as the original series of episodes shown here.

Agnes nods and says, "I think they were trying to pitch it to an American audience this time, and they didn't realize that the very thing Americans loved about it was that it was so *British.*"

Besides that, purely in terms of the writing, she feels too many story lines were dropped without being sufficiently dramatized.

"Take Lizzie, the daughter—we hear the other characters talk about how she has fallen in love, married a man, and gone off to America. But I wanted to *see* Lizzie falling in love, I wanted to *see* the man she married. It's not enough just to be *told* she fell in love and got married and went to America."

We are warming up to the subject of storytelling, talking of movies and plays we've enjoyed or found disappointing. This is the continuing subject in Agnes' house—the telling of stories and the talking about the telling of them, and in different ways it continues at dinner.

The dining room is lit with many candles, not only on the table but also set around the room, flickering warmly against the dark-brown wallpaper that Agnes says they were going to have removed because it was so dark until they learned it was original French provincial, rare and valuable. It is warmed now by the candlelight, which also illuminates two imposing portraits of "store-bought ancestors." Agnes found them in antique shops and thought they'd look nice in this room. One is of a dark-haired nineteenth-century gentleman who was a U.S. senator from Mississippi. The other is a lovely darkhaired woman whose face bears some resemblance to that of the senator, but her identity is unknown. Agnes just thought she'd go well with the senator.

Agnes and Bob and I are joined around the table by their daughter Mary, Mary's daughter Ceara, and their daughter Emily. There is a huge roast beef, mashed potatoes, broccoli, salad, and for dessert the Concord-grape pie that Agnes serves for special occasions. It is the best kind of All-American meal, hearty and honest and plentiful, a family kind of meal.

I am sitting next to Emily, the youngest of the children, a bright and pretty seventeen-year-old with pale white skin and straight blond hair. Emily tells me she's a senior at the Baldwin School and she's preparing her auditions for the drama departments of colleges she's applied to enter the following fall. Alvina Kraus, her mother's old drama teacher, now retired, is coming to spend a weekend soon and help Emily with her preparations for auditioning.

Agnes says Emily had a very *early* audition experience as a child, and asks, "Em, do you mind if I tell about it?"

Emily shrugs and says no, she doesn't mind Agnes telling that story any more.

Agnes says when Emily was two years old, and of course a beautiful baby, she used to carry her picture around, and one day she showed it to someone in television who was so impressed he asked Agnes if she'd like to bring the baby around to audition for a television commercial for children's toys.

"I was so proud," Agnes remembers, "and I got Em all dressed up, and took her to the studio. The director got her in front of the camera playing with the toy, cute as could be, and I was standing in the background beaming, and just at the *precise* moment the director gave the sign to start shooting, Em stuck a finger up her nose. The director yelled 'Cut!' and that was it. The audition was over."

By the time we get to the pie the story talk gets back to soap operas, and I learn that Em and Mary are faithful followers of "All My Children," and so is Agnes' daughter Cathy, who is married to a graduate student at Northwestern. The only one of Agnes' children who doesn't watch the show is her son Bobby, who works on a Wildlife Preserve in Maryland, is serious about ecology, and doesn't have a television set. I get the feeling he doesn't *want* to have one.

I mention a new soap that's supposed to be very hot right now, a competitor for the youthful viewers that "All My Children" attracts, and I ask if anyone has seen it and what they think of it.

Emily frowns and says, "No wonder they're doing so well, they're out in Hollywood, and they have all those pretty faces. And besides, they're copying from *us*."

Agnes says, "Emily!"

"Well, they are," Em says. "They have an older woman

who keeps looking in the mirror and pulling at her skin and I just bet now they're going to have her get a face lift, just like *Margo* did on 'All My Children.'"

Agnes says, "No, dear, they're not copying, and I don't think that woman's going to get a face lift. The writer is a very good storyteller, and he's had the woman and her husband toying with a gun, and I'll bet you anything someone's going to get killed. Otherwise they wouldn't be showing that gun so much."

After dinner, in the living room I ask Agnes if she watches many other soaps on a regular basis. She says she watches others from time to time, especially a new one that does very well, like the one we were talking about.

"I've watched it to try to see what quality it has that the audience finds attractive. It *is* good storytelling, but it's so—unrelieved in its tragedy. I like to have some lightness on the show. I love to have *Nick Davis* come on and make a crack about something. I like to see him come on camera in one of his *Nick*-like outfits with the belted jacket and shooting lapels, and deliver some good funny lines and have some laughs. Those are things that make life worthwhile to me—some lightness and good humor—and I want those things on the show."

I say one of the reasons I like "All My Children" is that it has such relief, that some of the soaps I've watched have such constant problems and tragedies they seem sort of—"frantic."

"Fraught," says Agnes. "You have to be careful of being too fraught."

I also mention some of the soaps seem depressing not only because of the stories but because of the sets and lighting.

"There's one," I say, "that looks like the people can't afford anything more than forty-watt bulbs and thrift-shop furniture. It looks kind of—tawdry or something."

"Tacky," says Agnes.

"*That's* it," I say.

Fraught and tacky.

That's what you want to avoid.

Agnes is a good listener as well as a good storyteller, and

after another Lillet I find myself telling her all about a movie script I wrote based on my last novel that seemed about to be produced and then fell through at the last moment. Agnes wonders if it might be right for a TV nighttime special, they're always looking for those. I say I really don't know, and she asks me, "Does it *build?*" and I say I really don't know, and she says with conviction, "Well, it's all right if a novel doesn't build, a novel is a whole other thing, but if it's going to be a TV movie it has to *build.*"

When we finished the Lillet I climb the stairs to the second-floor guest room and go to bed wondering whether or not my script in fact *builds.* . . . The word is ringing in my mind, as if it's the key to everything, certainly to everything that has to do with storytelling. I think of children with blocks. . . . I think of piling bricks on top of one another. . . . I vow that if I ever write a script again it will damn well *build.* . . .

Morning sounds.

Ceara calling. Muffled voice of an early radio news broadcast. Bacon frying. The broom-baroom of the green station wagon Bob drives to work as he warms up the motor in the driveway outside my window.

Clouds of smoke puff from the exhaust into the cold air. The day outside the window looks icy, making the warmth of the house more tangible and comfortable.

"This house gets up at seven-fifteen," Agnes has told me the night before, and I am up with it, enjoying the sense of its waking around me.

Sadie Gay, the Nixons' cook and housekeeper, prepares eggs to anyone's order. There is bacon and sausage on a warmer, orange juice and coffee. Everyone eats at his own pace, and everyone's newly wakened privacy is respected. You don't have to make conversation. Agnes is wearing a long maroon housecoat, woolly and comfortable-looking. After breakfast she will go to work in her third-floor study until ten, when her secretary, Rita Sulger, comes to the second-floor office off the guest room to type letters and story outlines and keep Agnes apprised of her schedule. In the coming weeks Agnes is going to talk to the students at the Irwin School, a girls' prep school in suburban Philadelphia, go to New York for conferences with the writers and production staff of "All My Children," go to Detroit for a taping of "The Lou Gordon Show" that will discuss soap opera, and to Ohio State University to speak before an anthropology seminar and an acting class that are using "All My Children" in their class work.

After having lunch and watching the show Agnes will return to writing and dictating and talking to the writers and producers and sometimes the actors on the telephone. I ask if she isn't bothered by the many interruptions of her work from the telephone and she says, "I'm used to it. You have to accept it—it's part of the turf. It comes with the territory."

Agnes comes down for lunch around half past twelve and I join her in the TV room, where Sadie brings us hamburgers and we eat and talk before the show comes on. Agnes is telling me how many effective things are done on the spur of the moment, on the set.

"For instance," she says, "in direction and camera work there's such a thing as 'playing to weakness.' There was one actor we had on the show who had particular trouble remembering his lines, and when he was trying to think of them he had this really tortured look on his face that was very dramatic. So if that matched the mood of the scene, they'd do a close-up of him. Bud Kloss said once, 'Just think, there are all those people out there thinking how soulful he looks, and actually he's struggling to remember his lines.'"

Yesterday's show had ended with the mounting suspense about the fate of *Little Phillip Tyler*, who will have to have an operation for his ruptured spleen, but the Prologue of today's program doesn't even deal with that, and concerns the mounting marital problems of *Margo* and her new husband, *Paul Martin*. I ask if this is intentional, and Agnes says, "Not necessarily. I tell the writers the main thing for the Prologue is to do something interesting, get people to watch, then worry about everything else later."

Little Phillip is not mentioned in Act I, nor in the beginning of Act II, but in the middle of Act II the scene switches from *Margo* and *Paul* to the hospital where *Little Phillip's* relatives are gathered to hear more news of his condition.

I ask Agnes why the *Little Phillip* story is brought back in the middle of a scene, instead of waiting to begin the next scene with it. She explains that "most of yesterday's show was about *Little Phillip,* and I was afraid that if we didn't get back to his story *before* the third commercial break, people might turn off. They might not be ready to sit through the next commercial if they didn't think they'd find out something more about *Little Phillip.*"

Not everything, though, is designed to keep the viewers in a constant stranglehold of plot. Agnes says she is planning a scene for when the weather gets better this spring in which *Little Phillip* will be taken out kite flying.

"This will be one of the few exterior scenes we've had in a long time. It's not so important to the story but I think it's important to us on the show, especially the writers. After a while you begin to get 'writing claustrophobia,' knowing that all the scenes have to be inside."

I am writing this in my notebook but suddenly I stop, swivel in my chair, and point a finger at Agnes.

"Aha!" I say. "You slipped! I know you try not to give away what will happen next, but now I know *Little Phillip* is going to recover from his injury and be all right, because he's going out kite flying in the spring!"

Agnes looks dismayed for a moment, then smiles, swivels her chair away, and says, "Well, I said he'd go outdoors and help fly a kite, and of course that means he's not going to *die—*"

"Yes!"

Agnes swivels back toward me, her eyes wide and mischievous, and, pointing a finger at *me*, says, "But I never said *Little Phillip* would ever play the violin again!"

We both laugh. Agnes wins again. No. We all win. We want to know what happens next.

We want to know the story.

TELLING
THE STORY

Agnes happens to be on one of her few visits to the set when an actor comes up waving his script and says, "Agnes, I can't say this line."

Agnes looks at the line and asks why not.

The actor explains it has him telling his wife he'll toss the salad for dinner. He says he can't do that.

"You can't toss a salad?" Agnes asks.

"No, I mean my character couldn't do that—he *wouldn't* do that."

Agnes asks why not.

"Because it's not masculine," the actor says. "The next thing you know, you'll have him scrubbing the kitchen floor."

Agnes writes a compromise. She has the character say he'll toss the salad, but adds a line that allows him to say in complaint of that act, "Next thing you know, you'll have me scrubbing the kitchen floor."

The actor feels the compromise salvages the masculinity of the character he plays, and Agnes thinks the line is funny. As well as the situation.

But having the writer change lines on the spot for the actor takes time and effort and does not always result in an agreeable compromise. That's one of many reasons Agnes doesn't feel it's wise to spend a lot of time on the set, even when she's in New York.

"But really the main thing is," she says, "the cast and production people are terribly busy, and that's not where I belong. I usually only go over there for an 'occasion'—like when there's a 'wedding' in the story, which means all the cast will be there that day, or for parties, like the one we had to celebrate the taping of our thousandth show, and the Christmas party we have every year.

"I think the cast is great. I'm really impressed by what I see them do. It's an ensemble effort in the truest sense of the word."

And Agnes, as the creator and writer, is a very real part of that ensemble, immeasurably more so than, say, the writer of a movie who may never even meet the actors whose lines he has written, whose connection with cast and production may well be over when he hands in his finished script. But for Agnes, for any creator-writer of a daytime television serial, that's when the vital relationship with the actors really begins.

"After you've created the characters in your presentation for a serial," Agnes explains, "and after the show goes on the air, those characters that were born out of your imagination become 'real people' played by actors and actresses. And those actors and actresses, in the way they look and the way they play their parts, feed the imagination of the writer to such a degree that lots of new ideas come into being.

"In a strange way, the actors help to write the show. I'll give you a perfect example. In the original story projection of 'All My Children,' *Nick Davis* was supposed to die at the end of six months. But when Larry Keith came on playing *Nick*, and that screen lit up with Larry on it, with all the subtleties and nuances and complexities of character he brought to the part, I thought, 'We can't lose this one!' you know."

And Larry Keith as *Nick Davis* is still in the show now, six years later, and still changing, in ways that come about through the actor as well as the writer. Like Larry telling

Agnes he'd like to sing on the show and Agnes "giving him" a nightclub. And the way that Larry has "played against" the pure-villain character of *Nick* as it was originally conceived, making him more of a "cad" than a simple "baddie," and turning him now increasingly into a more sympathetic cad, one who not only is a victimizer but also is victimized. Agnes admits this "change in his character" has partly come about because Larry plays *Nick* so sympathetically that "he's got me going along with it, writing to it."

This of course is a creative instance of the relationship of writer and actor changing the course of the story, but obviously changes in the plot also come about from less happy circumstances. As Larry's part was "written in" to the continuing story line because of his excellent performance, inevitably there are characters who have to be "written out" when the actor or actress simply doesn't fulfill the expectations of the writers, producers, and directors who must keep the show on the air.

If it's decided that a character must be written out, the writers can of course determine when in the story it will happen, can plan long-term plots around the departure, and select the means of his demise. He may not be "killed off" at all but just sent away to start a business in Seattle or go on an archaeological dig in Samarkand. That leaves open the possibility of bringing the "character" back in the form of another actor who, after a suitable period of time for the audience not to be shocked or confused by a "new Archibald," or whoever, can simply return to Pine Valley. If, however, the character seems dispensable to the continuing story, or if an actor can't be found who seems like a good replacement for the original in this particular role, then it can be revealed that poor Archibald has drowned while salmon fishing in Seattle or has expired of sunstroke in Samarkand.

It is far more difficult for the writers when a character has to be written out because the actor for whatever reason wants to leave the program. Temporary leaves of absence for being on tour with a national theater company as Ruth Warrick was with *Irene*, or for having a baby as Susan Lucci did, can be written "around" by having *Phoebe* go off on her round-the-world cruise, or *Erica* have a miscarriage and then a mental breakdown that sent her off to Oakhaven, a private sanitarium. But when an actor in the story wants to go for good, the writers have a real dilemma. And it's an increasingly common one.

Michael Brockman, ABC's vice-president in charge of daytime programming, says the problem of keeping actors is one of the most important factors in the success of a serial:

"The word 'commitment' is a big thing here—for an audience to identify with a character takes a long time, six months or a year. It takes at least two years for an actor to be productive in terms of the show. And the young talent just don't want to make that time commitment."

Most often the actor leaves because of a better job, or, in the case of many younger people, because of the hope of making it on Broadway or in the movies, the desire to try their luck on the stage or in Hollywood.

Mary Fickett, the actress who plays nurse *Ruth Martin,* has been in Broadway plays and movies and is sympathetic to the young people who want to make their bid for the big time. She says, "The younger people who haven't yet been in movies or theater 'want their turn,' and I understand how they feel. Like the original *Tara, Chuck,* and *Phil.*"

And now *Jeff* and *Mary.*

Agnes sympathizes, too, but that doesn't make it any easier for her when Charlie Frank and Susan Blanchard announce their simultaneous departure from Pine Valley to the more glamorous and potentially more rewarding town of Hollywood.

The manner of how they are written out of course depends on who they are and what they've been doing in the story, and in telling me how she plans to "dispose" of them, Agnes tells the history of these particular roles and these particular actors.

Charlie Frank plays the handsome and good-hearted young *Dr. Jeff Martin,* and the audience has grieved for the poor guy as he suffered through his marriage to the bitchy *Erica Kane.*

Once out of that marriage, it was obvious that *Jeff* deserved something better, that it was only right and just that he find a good woman, one who in contrast to *Erica* would be sweet of disposition and simple in her needs, a genuine homebody who would give *Jeff* the kind of home and family he so richly deserved.

In Agnes' long-term story projection, written every six months (with addendums to update it), she looks ahead from the *Jeff-Erica* relationship while it is still going on to see that "far down the road, but inexorably, the day will come when *Jeff* realizes that all his efforts to help *Erica* become a whole person, a complete woman, have failed and he will then meet and fall in love with a real woman, a woman of warmth, humor, and understanding. . . ."

When this woman "comes along" in the next story projection, she is a registered nurse named *Mary Kennicott,* and Agnes creates her character and appearance and even her past as follows:

"Reared on a farm outside Hazleton, Pennsylvania, the second oldest of eight children, with many more deprivations than luxuries, *Mary Kennicott* is the complete antithesis of *Erica Kane.* . . ."

Whereas *Erica* is the spoiled, self-absorbed, and selfish siren, *Mary* will be the warm, wholesome homebody, exuding warmth and trust. The part of *Mary* is superbly cast with Susan Blanchard, a freckle-faced, wide-eyed, short-haired, soft-voiced, and talented young actress who can, in the blink of her eyes, make everyone believe that virtue and innocence are still abroad in the land.

The long-term story plan is that:

"*Mary* will be introduced in early spring simply as a member of the hospital staff so that the audience will get to know her before *Jeff* does and we can avoid 'telegraphing' of story which so often occurs when a new character is introduced at the moment when the viewer is expecting a romantic complication."

Mary will then be assigned to the same floor of the Pine

Valley Hospital where *Dr. Jeff* works, and they will meet, and slowly but surely, fall in love.

What isn't in the long-term story projection is that while the characters *Jeff* and *Mary* fall in love, so do the actors playing them, Charlie and Susan.

Soon *Afternoon TV* magazine is headlining: "Charles Frank and Susan Blanchard—Their unforgettable love story will warm your heart."

Charlie, shaking his head and smiling as he discusses the whole thing, tells me that "sometimes I have the feeling Agnes is 'writing my life.'"

But now the roles are reversed, at least in the sense that Charlie and Susan by going off to Hollywood and leaving the show are determining the fates of the characters they play, *Jeff* and *Mary*.

At least they are determining that *Jeff* and *Mary* will leave the show, but it's up to Agnes to figure out how and why.

The difficulties of writing out *Jeff* and *Mary* are compounded by other factors in the Pine Valley story. Before Charlie and Susan decided to leave, Agnes was considering the possibility of another character being killed off, but that has to be changed now. We are suddenly dealing with three potential deaths in one small community, and that is altogether too many.

Unless itinerant Mafia henchmen come in and shoot up the Château Nick Davis, or a 747 jetliner bound for Seattle crashes into the Pine Valley Hospital. . . . No. Agnes doesn't want more than one death to strike the town in a short span of time.

Agnes decides that *Mary* will be the one to be killed off, but now she has to figure out how it happens and that is especially complicated in this case because of *Mary's* "back story."

Agnes has worked into the character of *Mary* a long-term story line involving her having leukemia, but eventually being cured. The idea of this came from Agnes' reading Stewart Alsop's book *Stay of Execution,* and she further researched the subject of leukemia and found there are now successful treatments of the disease. The audience does not yet know *Mary* has leukemia, but they know of certain symptoms she has shown and of some kind of illness and worried fan letters have expressed concern about *Mary's* health while others have warned the writers against "killing her off" because they like her and suspect this is being planned.

So one of Agnes' options is to reveal that *Mary* has had leukemia all along and have the poor girl die of the disease.

"But I can't do that," Agnes tells me, "because I don't want to scare people. The whole point of this story line was going to be to give hope to people who have leukemia or have relatives or friends or loved ones who have it, to show them there are treatments now that help or cure the disease and you don't necessarily have to die of it. If I had *Mary* die of it just for the sake of the story line, I'd be doing just the opposite of what I originally intended."

I know that Agnes' concern about such things is genuine. I know among other reasons because I was looking through a bunch of scripts once that were sent her by the dialogists and on which she added her editorial comments. There was one script in which *Mona Kane,* in distress, is asking *Dr. Charles Tyler* about the effects of her daughter *Erica* having electric-shock treatments at the Oakhaven sanitarium, and one line is crossed out. The script had *Mona* say about her fear of the treatments, "They're given over and over again until the patient comes to dread them."

Agnes had written in the margin beside that line, "I'd omit this . . . it won't help anyone."

Having rejected death by leukemia, Agnes decides *Mary* will die in a car accident. That could happen to anyone. To the extent that it scares anyone, it will only have the effect of making them drive more carefully.

But Agnes isn't altogether happy with the idea of killing off *Mary* in a car accident. Her main reservation is that because of the limitations of production and budget you couldn't show a car crash on daytime television. You would just have to have someone rush into a room and *say* it happened. And Agnes knows that nothing that is reported secondhand is nearly as dramatic as something the audience can witness for itself.

Around this time, there are stories in the Philadelphia papers about a man and his son going up and down the East Coast getting into people's houses by some ruse or other and then murdering and robbing the people. It occurs to Agnes that *Mary's* trusting character, which makes her charmingly naïve, could also lead her to let a stranger into her house. That is a dangerous practice and in *Mary's* case it will be fatal, for the stranger is an escaped convict, and he will panic when he thinks *Mary* is signaling for help and will shoot and kill her.

This is not only a dramatic way for *Mary* to be killed off, but it also has a message: Be careful of strangers who come to your door, and for goodness' sake don't let them inside! Even in Pine Valley, such a practice can be not only dangerous but fatal.

Now having disposed of *Mary*, we come to *Jeff*. Agnes feels it would be too painful to have both him and *Mary* killed off, that the audience would simply find that too depressing if not also too incredible. So *Jeff*, in his understandable anguish over the death of his beloved young wife, is someday after the tragedy simply going to move to a one-doctor town where the doctor is ill and, at the same time, leave Pine Valley and his own painful memories of their life there together.

Drastic as it is for a character to leave Pine Valley, it's not as bad as dying, and the departure leaves open the possibility of his return—though of course with a new actor and after enough time has elapsed so the viewers won't be shocked by seeing a "new *Jeff*." In the long-term story projection Agnes says to her writers in an aside: Let's hope there's a "Mr. Right" somewhere out there to come on as *Jeff*.

And, though she didn't say so, I imagine she was also hoping that the new "Mr. Right" who plays *Jeff* does not fall in love with his romantic lead in the story and go off with her into Sunset Boulevard.

But this is one of the major calculations in the maze of factors involved in writing a continuing serial that runs five days a week all year for an unlimited number of years: the "characters" in the story you are writing are alive. They get sick, get married, get mad, get restless, get pregnant, get other offers, fall in love, fall off horses, fall apart, come together, go away, come back again.

Agnes hears about all those things and more, as she must, in order to work them into or out of the story as the case may be.

"The phone is always ringing," she says. "Mary Fickett wants to be away on a particular day to take her daughter Bronwyn to the first day of school. Francesca James is going to play Shaw in St. Louis. Susan Lucci is pregnant."

And Agnes gets a card from Ruth Warrick while she's touring with *Irene* that says, "By the way, *Phoebe* has a new hairdo—short and *chic*—so maybe we better write it in."

Until a few years ago Agnes did her writing at a long table with a lamp and an electric typewriter set up in the master bedroom, but now she has what every writer wants—her own private study to work in. She works at a desk surrounded by her own mementos and photographs, favorite books and reference works, a bulletin board for clippings and messages of current interest. She has an easy chair to rest in; she can leaf through a book or magazine or just sit back and close her eyes on those inevitable occasions during every workday when a writer thinks his brain is going to burst if he doesn't get his mind off what he's trying to write for a while.

The room is cozy, with a slanting roof and crank-out windows that give it a garret-like feeling, the sense of a hideaway, a private aerie. In one small alcove are three framed samplers done by her grandmother Katie Ryan, and on the wall and to the left of her desk hangs a Bachrach photograph of Irna Phillips; both, in their own way, "ancestors." In a bookcase behind the desk is a whole shelf of volumes devoted to her maternal national ancestry: *A Treasury of Irish Folklore* by Padraic Colum, *Irish Journal* by Heinrich Böll, *The Irish* by Sean O'Faolain, *The American Irish* by William Shannon, *Real Lace* by Stephen Birmingham, *The Irish Mystique* by Max Caulfield. On another shelf are novels, books on movies, theater, and television, autobiographies by Enid Bagnold and

Dorothy Parker. There is also a large volume which I realize
is probably essential for a writer of a daytime television serial:
Dorland's Illustrated Medical Dictionary. There's a copy of
the classic children's book *The Little Red Hen*, given to Agnes
by her husband Bob because the Little Red Hen is the one
who always says, as Agnes does, "I'll do it myself!" There is
also the gold cup she was awarded for "special contribution
to daytime TV" by the magazine *Afternoon TV*, a much worn
edition of the Jerusalem Bible, and a carved wooden cross. On
the desk are individual color photos of all her children.

Agnes also has in her study something I've never seen before, and I tell her right off that it makes me jealous. I want
one, too. This coveted object is a tan reclining chair, but it is
not just *any* reclining chair. It *does* things. You sit down and
lie back in it, adjusting it to your desired angle of repose, and
then with a knob on the right you can start it vibrating, at any
velocity you wish, and with the twist of a knob on the left you
can cause warm air to start blowing up out of the chair. This
chair does everything but write for you.

To the left of the chair is a small Sony portable color TV
and a Norelco tape recorder with microphone that she speaks
her ideas into for story outlines, and, to the right, leaning
against the wall is a wooden-and-wicker breakfast tray, like
the ones in thirties movies that were brought to glamorous
society ladies by maids who opened the draperies to let in the
late-morning sun and then served Madame breakfast in bed.
But Agnes doesn't use the tray for such decadent purpose. She
puts it across her lap and uses it (as a sort of portable table
desk) to write on. The first part of her writing process is
"roughing out" the day's story outline on a long yellow legal
pad placed on the breakfast tray, and later she will dictate
into the microphone and have that typed up, and then rewrite
and edit it and have that version retyped and sent to the
dialogists.

When a student asks her once how long that process takes,
how long it takes to do one daily outline, Agnes says, "Well,
you know, it depends on how fast the ideas are coming. Also,
sometimes you get into a story that's moving well and events

seem to start writing themselves. But even so, how long it takes depends on a lot of different things that don't have anything directly to do with writing. It depends on how much sleep you got the night before, whether you have a cold or sinus trouble, or if you're worried about something else. It depends on how many times the phone rings, it depends on whether you go to a parents' meeting at the Baldwin School and don't get back until late. But I would say, in general, that from the time I sit down with that yellow legal pad and write out in pencil what I think should happen, and go over it, and dictate the daily outline, I'd say that on a good day that takes two hours. But it can take anywhere from one to five hours. Two hours would be a good day."

But of course the reality of the daily outline comes long after the successful creation of the show, and its acceptance by a network, and finally its getting on the air.

It all begins with the Bible.

I don't mean the King James version or the Jerusalem Bible that Agnes has in her study.

The Bible is what Agnes calls the presentation or proposal for a TV serial. It is comparable to what is known in Hollywood as the "treatment" for a movie script. The Bible for a daytime serial includes a description of the story's locale, a cast of characters with extensive backgrounds and personality sketches for each one, followed by a long-term story projection of fifty to a hundred pages which tells what will happen in the story during the first year, and then the first five scripts that would begin the program.

That is what you begin with and what you go back to for information and inspiration. It is the foundation of the world of your story.

An opening part of the Bible of "All My Children" actually was mistaken once for a passage from the real Bible. There was an epigraph on the very first page, a lyrical statement of the theme of the story that said:

". . . The great and the least, the weak and the strong, in joy and sorrow, in hope and fear, in tragedy and triumph, you are all my children."

Someone from ABC called Agnes and asked what part of the Old Testament that was taken from. She explained that she wrote it herself.

Well it *does* have the rolling cadence of Old Testament prose. And it no doubt put the network executives who read it in a respectful frame of mind.

Once the story is accepted and under way the creator and/or head writer starts the daily outlines which go to dialogists or script writers. The outlines condense the action and feeling desired in a particular scene, which the script writer translates into dialogue (and then is given final editing by Agnes). A typical scene from a daily outline gives the following information and instruction:

"We return to them (*Phil* and *Erica*) finishing their dinner, perhaps having a brandy with their coffee. And the point and purpose of this scene—particularly the purpose—is to make the audience even more conciliatory and sympathetic toward *Erica*. . . . So again develop it as you wish but the thrust of it is her being humbly grateful and happy—without being saccharine or groveling—over the fact that *Phillip* wanted to marry her."

So the dialogist is given not just the who and where by the *why* of the scene, and is able to aim the lines he writes with that in mind. Sometimes, also, the daily outline contains more over-all guidelines as to the writing and development of the story, as in this "Note" signed "A.N." preceding a particular outline:

"This is a script which, though it doesn't contain high histrionics, is very important in that it progresses the relationship of *Charles* and *Mona* and that of *Linc* and *Kitty*. It also deals with *Paul* and *Margo* but the former two are more important because it is a stage which will then allow for further development. Of course, there shouldn't be giant steps taken in this one script, as I know you understand very well, its being very much an iceberg thing. But I just thought it was well to point out, not only for the writer but for Production as well, the importance of this script even though it is low-key because, since these scripts are so necessary over the months and years of a serial, they need to be given as much, if not more attention and care than those of high drama."

The outline may also, after describing a scene, emphasize the long-range role of a character in the story, not in the drama itself but in the character's relation to the audience:

". . . *Ruth* is one of the truth speakers in our cast of characters, even when she is forecasting something. In other words if *Ruth* has a 'feeling' about something the audience tends to take it as an indication of what may possibly happen. . . ."

Sometimes the outline includes a note of warning not to reveal too much, as after a scene in which *Lincoln Tyler* is talking to his sister *Anne* about what a fine person *Kitty Shea* is. He has just recently met *Kitty*, and he will eventually fall in love with her and marry her, but at this point the audience is still supposed to be guessing about that, perhaps hoping it will happen but not really sure, and the outline cautions:

". . . *Linc* himself consciously thinks he's relating this to *Anne* for *Anne's* sake more than because of his feelings about *Kitty* personally. Of course he does indeed think *Kitty* is everything he's saying but we just don't want to have this romance off and running at this point. I feel Production has already indicated a little too much just in the acting and so I don't want to get ahead of ourselves."

In addition to guidance provided in daily outlines, the long-term story projection, as well as setting up the long-range developments of the plot for the dialogists to have in mind as they write the daily scripts, also instructs and advises about over-all problems and policies. A long-term story projection notes after talking about what lies ahead for *Kitty Shea* that "in the day-to-day scripts, not a great deal will be made of the past relationship of *Kitty* with *Nick* because it would just get us too bogged down with unnecessary redundancy of past story."

And then the general policy about "past story" and the reasons behind it are explained:

"It is almost axiomatic that as a show gets older—and particularly when one wants to use the same characters who, portrayed by skilled actors, have contributed so much to the show's popularity—then one simply must start 'lopping off' some of the earlier relationships in terms of discussing or referring to them, as the necessity of covering them would put a terrible burden on the dialogue and be devastating to the pace of the individual shows and over-all progression of story. This is not to say that we should go counter to situations or *deny* that they existed but we should simply not discuss them.

"A prime example of this is the fact that *Phillip's* natural mother was married to *Lincoln Tyler*. I cannot foresee the day when we shall want to bring *Amy* back and therefore there is no present or future benefit to be derived from pointing up that ancient history. Yes, we can still say—when necessary— that *Nick* is *Phil's* natural father, that his mother was *Ruth's* sister, that *Ruth* adopted *Phillip*, etc., but the connection with *Linc* can certainly be overlooked since that whole *Amy* story was designed for a six-month period with Rosemary Prinz and built into the original plotting was the elimination of her at the end of that half-year mark. . . . Another bit of pre-show history which we are forgetting is the matter of *Anne's* having been married as a debutante to a French nobleman."

My God. *Anne* married as a debutante to a French nobleman?

That indeed is the sort of thing it's best not to bring up again.

And as if all this weren't enough to keep in mind, Agnes has to also refer all the time to the Dead Sea Scrolls.

She calls it that not because it's sacred, but because it's so hard to decipher.

She hands me a copy and I see what she means.

It is a piece of standard-sized typing paper, divided into squares. Penciled into each square in Agnes' handwriting are notes on the cast and sets and action for each day's episode. In the margins beside the squares each actor is "owed" according to his contract. If you don't use the actors for the number of performances they have contracted for, they get paid the same amount of money anyway, and in the Scrooge-like budget of soap opera, nothing can be wasted.

In addition to preparing and keeping track of all these written documents, Agnes talks with her writers on the phone and in person at meetings in New York.

"We have story conferences four times a year," Agnes says, "with all the writers, the directors, and the producer. These are real 'lemon sessions.' By that I mean everyone lays it on the line. Everyone says what they think hasn't worked, what was a lemon. There's no room for fragile egos at these meetings. We all have to say what we mean, come out with what's bothering us.

"We talk about plot of course, but we talk about character, too. For instance, we've discussed the personality of *Erica* and how she suffers not because she's a bad person but a neurotic one, and how she brings this suffering on herself by her own actions."

Agnes' writers come from a variety of daytime serial experience, and so are aware of the problems from personal knowledge of different aspects of a show's production.

Mary K. Wells was an actress on "The Edge of Night."

Kiki McCabe is an old friend of Agnes' who worked as her secretary typing scripts until Agnes one day said, "You type them all the time, why don't you try writing them?" Kiki did—and does.

Jack Wood was the original director of "All My Children." He left the show to go to Europe and work on a novel. Now he writes scripts for the program while he continues work on his book.

Wisner Washam's knowledge of daytime serials originally derived from his being married to a woman who works in them. His wife is Judith Barcroft, the actress who plays *Anne Tyler* in "All My Children."

Of course Wisner has other qualifications, but being married to an actress on the show you write for is a good start.

In the past year Agnes asked Wisner to help her write the daily outlines as well as do scripts.

"Now Wisner and I work very closely together," Agnes says. "I used to do all the daily outlines and now Wis does a lot of them, too. He and I talk on the phone about over-all story, and he does a rough draft of an outline while talking on the phone with me, or if I'm in New York we get together and work on it. Then he dictates it and sends it to a typist, and I get that version and edit it, and send it to be retyped, and it goes out to the dialogists."

Wisner is being groomed.

"My being here is a fluke," Wisner says, referring to his position as Agnes' main writer on "All My Children."

But luckily when I talk to Wisner, his lovely actress wife, Judith Barcroft, is there, so his modesty is tempered by her pride in him.

When Wisner tells me, "I'm very fortunate, Agnes has taught me so much about writing," Judith smiles and comments, "You were pretty good anyway."

I like that. And I like being in the Washams' living room this pleasant Sunday afternoon. They live on Riverside Drive in New York in the upper Eighties in a large, sunny apartment that seems both comfortable and elegant. When *Anne Tyler*, played by Judith, moves out of her parents' home and gets an apartment by herself in Pine Valley, she decorates it in much this manner of tasteful comfort, and her visitors comment how much the place "looks like *Anne*." So does this place—or maybe I should say it "looks like Judith."

Wisner is a handsome fellow with black hair and heavy black eyebrows, Southern in manner and accent—not corn-pone Southern, but gracious Southern, traditional Southern. He was raised in Virginia and North Carolina, and after graduating from the University of North Carolina at Chapel Hill he came to New York City.

"My goal was to be an actor," he says, "and like most people, I failed."

But unlike most people, he stayed on and made a living in the theater, working as a Broadway stage manager. He worked on four successive Neil Simon plays and in one of them, *Plaza Suite*, he met an actress named Judith Barcroft, who was an understudy for one of the parts, and he married her.

After the run of Neil Simon plays the only thing Wisner could find was a job as stage manager of a pretty far-off-Broadway show. Judith was pregnant and they needed money, so Wisner tried getting production jobs on soap operas, since Judith had worked on "Another World" as an actress and they knew some people on soaps. But he had no luck getting the sort of stage or production work he'd done in the theater, so Judith suggested he try writing for the soaps.

"I'd read some of the stories he'd written in college," she says, "and I thought they were quite good."

Wis wrote some sample scripts based on "Another World" because he'd watched that one when Judith worked on it and was familiar with the characters. He sent around the scripts and got a nice reply from Agnes, whom he and Judith had recently met socially. She gave him a trial, having him write one script a week. That was in January 1971, and he started writing regularly later that year.

"July," says Judith. "It was July 11, 1971."

Soon after, Judith herself joined the show.

I realize I have a rare opportunity to get both sides of the story of actor and writer, since here is one married to one, and both are working on the same program.

Judith says, "All actors complain about the writers. I was the same. I never realized till Wis started writing for 'All My Children' how difficult it is. It's like an incredible crossword puzzle. Actors tend to think the writing must be easy, but I know differently now. Wis works from nine to six almost every day."

Wis says, "I don't go to the studio much, except when they're auditioning new actors and actresses. Agnes believes in a certain degree of detachment of the writers from the actors, and I do believe that's best. With the exception, of course, that I live with this actress right here. But it is difficult for a writer to be around the actors a lot—in social situations there can really be a lot of pressure. Sometimes they want to tell you what should happen, and sometimes they want to know what's going to happen to the characters they play."

Judith is nodding emphatically and says, "I have to be the

7. Ruth Warrick sent this photo while on tour with the national company of *Irene* to her friends back in "Pine Valley," saying she was eager to be back home with them again in her role as socialite *Phoebe Tyler*.

8. Kay Campbell, who "grew up" in radio as *Ma Perkins'* daughter *Effie*, is now the wise grandmother *Kate Martin* on "All My Children."

9. Mary Fickett in the kitchen of her own home after a hard day playing the nicest person in the world, nurse *Ruth Martin*.

10. Producer Bud Kloss gets a rare few moments of peace and quiet at a late-morning lunch break in his booth at McGlade's restaurant.

11. Family within a family: Wisner Washam is a writer for "All My Children," his wife Judith Barcroft plays *Anne Tyler*, and their son Ian appears as *Little Phillip* in the show; baby daughter Amy is not yet old enough to have a role (at the time of this writing).

best secret keeper in town. So many people try to ask me what's going to happen that I'd really rather not know, it makes it easier if Wis doesn't even tell me. Also, sometimes the other actors will tell me things they *wish* would happen to them in the script, and I know they really want me to tell Wis, but I just nod and don't commit myself."

"It's an old tradition in soaps that actors aren't told the long-term plot," Wisner says.

"I know," Judith says, "and some actors like it that way, but I personally feel it's a mistake. It's like playing Blanche DuBois, and not knowing you're going to go crazy in the end."

Judith excuses herself to go see what their son is up to, and Wisner tells me more about the complexities of soap writing, of keeping track of what inevitably becomes a growing cast of characters, and all their relationships. The process Agnes described in her long-term story projection as "lopping off" helps simplify things. And sometimes things are simplified by accident. Wis tells the most famous case of disappearance in "All My Children," concerning *Joe Martin's* son *Bobby*. I remember reading about the character *Bobby* in "the Bible" and I've been curious about what happened to him.

Wis tells me that "one night Bobby went upstairs to polish his skis—and he's never been heard from since. I guess the writers forgot, and he wasn't important in the plot anyway, and it was more complicated to explain his disappearance than to just forget it. It's a standing joke among the cast. Every once in a while someone will say, 'Hey, where's *Bobby?*' and Ray MacDonnell, who supposedly plays his father, will snap his fingers and say, 'Where the hell did that kid go?' and maybe someone will yell, '*Bobby!* Has anyone seen *Bobby* around?'"

Judith comes back in the living room holding the hand of a small, blond, curly-headed boy. Judith smiles and asks if I know who this is.

"Of course I know," I say. "That's *Little Phillip*. I just saw him playing in the inflatable swimming pool in Grandma *Kate's* back yard last week."

Besides being *Little Phillip* on "All My Children," the boy is Ian Washam, Wis and Judith's son.

"He loves going to the studio," Judith says, "but I don't want him to do it too much. I don't want to be a stage mother. I've seen too many children get spoiled on sets, get fed too much Coca-Cola and candy and everything else."

And Ian, Judith, and Wis are not the only members of the family who have worked on soaps. I don't mean their new daughter Amy, although her christening was covered in the soap fan magazines. But she's still too small to go to the studio. The other soap performer in the family is Judith's father, the Very Reverend J. L. Barcroft. When Judith was on "Another World" her father conducted a funeral service on the show when one of the characters died.

"It was a beautiful service," Wis says. "I knew the casket was empty but I still felt like crying, I was so moved."

He pauses a moment and says, reflectively, "We haven't had a funeral yet on our show. But if we ever do . . ."

Some of the problems of writing a soap are much the same as problems in any other form of storytelling.

One of these is that people always ask, "Where do you get your ideas?" After posing that question to Agnes some students ask her if she gets her ideas from her friends, and if they are worried that she is writing about them.

"Not my good friends, no," she says. "They know I'm not writing about them—because a writer's mind doesn't work that way. You just, you know, something will spark an idea, maybe even a person will set it off—but no parts are taken wholecloth. I mean, it goes through a writer's mind, you take a little bit from that person, a little bit from this person, and you know, people write not only from their experiences but from their dreams and imagination. Look at the Brontë sisters. They never left the rectory, and, you know, look at the things they wrote, just out of their dreams and imagination. . . ."

Agnes tells me her own favorite writers are Kay Boyle and Katherine Anne Porter.

"I enjoy other writers," she says, "like Faulkner and Eudora Welty, but I don't feel the same affinity for them that I do for Kay Boyle and Katherine Anne Porter."

I ask if she has ever thought of writing something else, a play perhaps.

"No, not a play. I've been in the confines of a studio for so long now, I'd feel like it was too much of the same thing."

Nor is she interested in doing a movie script.

Agnes Nixon wants to write a novel.

That will have its own set of built-in problems and pressures, but at least they won't all be the same as the extraspecial pressures that come with writing a daytime TV serial.

Like the Ratings.

The Ratings seem inevitable, like death and taxes, but they come more often. They come every week.

A student at the Irwin School in Philadelphia asks Agnes if the Ratings are "true," which is something like asking if a mountain in front of your car is "true." It doesn't matter if it's true, what matters is it's *there*.

"Well, you know, it's always been a point of argument as to whether Nielsen's ratings are accurate," Agnes explains. "They—Nielsen—say they have Arbitron meters—or audio meters—in fourteen thousand homes, spanning economic, social, and geographic areas, and they say that the fourteen thousand is totally representative of all the people in the country. I'm not sure it is, but on the other hand I have to live by it and work by it."

Later I ask Agnes how immediate the effects of the ratings are; that is, does everyone start to panic if the show gets a bad rating just a few weeks in a row, or does it take a long period for the network to get edgy and finally cancel the program because of poor ratings.

"Any network knows it takes a long time for a soap to build," Agnes says. "The network knows a new show is bound to start low, but if they see a pattern of growth, they'll stick with it. They also take into consideration a writer's track record. If the writer has had successful shows before, they're more likely to stick it out with the same writer over a long period of time even if things aren't going well."

The Nielsens give statistics on a number of different aspects of a show's audience, and each category has two different figures. The first is the percentage of sets tuned to the program out of the total number of sets in the whole country. The second figure is called the "share" and it is the percentage of sets tuned to the program out of the total number of sets turned on during that time period.

Agnes shows me a monthly compilation (she receives ratings each week) of the Nielsen ratings for February 1975, that being the key month every year because it is the time of what is called the "peak-sets-in-use period." In other words, more people are watching daytime television then than in any other month of the year, and all the shows drum up the most dramatic story lines they can to peak in that month.

Harding Lemay, head writer of "Another World," tells me he made a point of studying what all the soaps were doing in February 1975, and found that out of fourteen serials on the air, six of them had courtroom trials going. Lemay didn't stage a courtroom trial, but he did have the wealthy and jealous socialite *Iris* trying to insidiously break up the engagement of her distinguished father, *Mac Corey*, to the younger, beautiful, but socially unprominent *Rachel Frame*.

"And it worked," Lemay says. "Our ratings went up."

The range of percentage figures for February 1975 in the Nielsens for the fourteen daytime serials went from 4.9 for "How to Survive a Marriage" at the bottom (which was canceled a few months later) to 9.2 for "All My Children" at the top. "All My Children" also was tops with 9.8 for audiences with $15,000-plus incomes, and tops with 7.0 for audiences with $20,000-plus incomes. It was number two in households with the head of household having one or more years of college education.

Agnes explains to me that "in the last five years the Nielsens can also tell what age group is watching and this is very important to the sponsors, this is what they're interested in."

In the Nielsen compilations of ratings according to age

group for April 1974 to March 1975, "All My Children" was
number one in categories of women aged 18–34 and women
aged 18–49.

Agnes says, "We have the highest rating in the 18–49
group, and that's what counts. If you have a huge audience
but it's mainly people over fifty, it's no go with the sponsors."

In addition to pressures from ratings, for the first five years
of "All My Children" and before that for the first five years of
"One Life to Live," Agnes had the added pressure of being,
along with her husband Bob, owner of the program through
their company, Creative Horizons, Inc. Through the company
they had packaged these programs, and then eventually sold
them to the network.

Under the arrangement in which Creative Horizons owned
and packaged the program, the "below the line" expenses
were handled by the ABC network—that is, the studio, the
sets, cameras, grips, costume designers, set designers, and all
"physical facilities." The network then paid Creative Horizons
to furnish the "above the line" elements, which mainly come
under the heading of "talent"—the producer, associate producers, production assistants, actors, writers, directors, casting
director.

"That's what a packager furnishes," Agnes explains. "It uses
the 'below the line' facilities of the network, the network gives
it the money to furnish the 'above the line' personnel, and the
network puts the show on the air.

"And," says Agnes, "it's a very tight ship."

And the longer the packager owns the show, the tighter the
ship becomes.

Creative Horizons, Inc. sold "All My Children" to ABC in
January 1975, and Agnes explains to me that:

"The longer you own the show, the more difficult it becomes, both financially and personally. The network allowed
in our contract a small increment in costs every year, but costs
of course are bound to go much higher. All actors feel they
deserve more than they're getting, and it's very unpleasant for
me to have to say no, especially when the actor is a personal
friend. Perhaps I should not make friends with actors, but

some of my dearest friends are people in the cast, like Mary Fickett, and I certainly wouldn't want to change that. Some people might thrive on the business part of running a show but I just cringe. Selling it to the network takes all that pressure off me, and that means more time and energy for the creative part."

And then there are new pressures.

There is great pressure on Agnes to make "All My Children" into an hour show. In January 1975 "Another World" went to an hour, and a few months later "Days of Our Lives" followed. The students at Ohio State ask Agnes and Stephanie Braxton if "All My Children" is going to an hour, and they answer with very firm conviction.

"As far as the hour goes," Agnes says, "I personally don't think it's a good idea. ABC asked me to have 'All My Children' go to an hour two years ago, and I told them, 'We don't want to get bigger—we want to get better.' I feel it would be an exquisite dilemma to try to do both. I mean, I think either the writing would suffer and you'd have to do a lot of padding —or you'd kill your cast, physically."

Stephanie agrees vehemently, saying, "One of the things that I think makes watching 'All My Children' a pleasure is that you can see the same people develop over a long period of time. If you're working your actors fourteen hours a day, day in and day out, I guarantee you're not going to get many actors who are going to stay more than a year, possibly two years. You can't do it. Whereas with the working schedule we have now, you can go on almost indefinitely, as an actor, without wearing out your machinery."

After two years of fighting off the hour format, in the spring of 1975 Agnes makes a concession. She agrees to do one week of hour shows to be aired during the month of June. One of the factors in her agreement to do it is that the network is putting "All My Children" into a new time slot, and the week of hour shows will help get the audience adjusted to the move.

The network wants to introduce a new soap opera called "Ryan's Hope," and they want to put it at 1 P.M., the old

"Children" time, since "Children" has been so successful and has established that half hour as a habit for many soap fans. So what then will they do with "All My Children"? The first thought is to put it at a time late in the afternoon when it will be against two soaps that are considered weak competition and are fairly low in the ratings. But Agnes fights against this proposal because of her belief that much of the "All My Children" audience is a "lunchtime audience" that includes a number of working men and women who watch the show on their lunch break and would not be able to watch it in mid or late afternoon. The next proposal is to put it at 12:30, which will provide a "lead-in" for the new soap, and keep "Children" still within lunch-hour viewing time. But it also means that "Children" must go against "Search for Tomorrow," the longest-running soap on the air, and one of the strongest, ranking second behind "Children" in those February Nielsens. Viewers who once might have watched both "Search" at 12:30 and "Children" at 1:00 will now have to choose between them. ABC has conducted research that shows "Children" has a very high "loyalty factor" among its fans, and they take this as a hopeful sign that "Children" can do well against "Search." But nobody really knows.

At any rate, by doing a week of hour shows that will go from 12:30 to 1:30, "Children" will first be seen in its new earlier time slot, and with a longer story that goes on through the old time slot, which hopefully will give "Children" a boost of attention and also pave the way for the new soap coming on the following week at 1:00.

When the week of hour shows is announced there is the predicted groaning from the cast, and the rumor quickly gets around that the show is going to go to an hour permanently, and there are threats of resignations if that really happens. Agnes goes to New York to meet with representatives of the cast and assure them it's only for a week and only because of the strategy involved in going to the new time slot.

While all this is going on I talk to Agnes on the phone and she sounds, understandably, weary.

"I told them O.K., I'll do it for a week and show you how

it's done—how it ought to be done. I'm not going to do it with long pauses and stretching the story out. I'm going to add new story, get a lot of different story lines moving, have a lot of action."

I point out that if she does all this, as I'm sure she can, it will bring more pressure on her to go to an hour permanently.

She says she simply won't do it.

But the pressure is there. Just another one of the pressures both constant and unexpected that bear upon the writer of a daytime TV serial.

By August the pressure of "going up against" the strong and popular "Search for Tomorrow" in the new "All My Children" time slot has considerably abated with the results of the latest Nielsens showing "Children," during and after its week of hour shows, gaining a higher rating than it enjoyed before the change, and at summer's end it is sitting firmly atop all daytime TV programs in the ratings.

But this doesn't mean Agnes can just sit back and relax.

The story must go on—and on. In early summer Agnes tells me she is working on a story line that will start to unfold in the fall and reach a climax the following January or February of 1976. It involves *Dr. Frank Grant,* and his wife *Nancy.* I am happy to hear this because I have asked Agnes before when and if *Frank* will get to do anything besides drink coffee with his friends and colleagues at the Pine Valley Hospital. I am worried that he may come down with caffeine poisoning.

Agnes explains that now with *Mary's* death and *Jeff's* leaving Pine Valley, "we have room now on the canvas to bring *Frank* and *Nancy* into the foreground." The audience will begin to see more of *Frank,* so that when his story comes up he will be "positioned for it," Agnes explains. She says, "When we bring in a story we want to have the audience so well acquainted with the characters and sympathetic to them that when the story occurs you've already won half the battle."

The *Frank-Nancy* story will not be a "racial" story, though they both are black. Rather, it will be a "women's lib" sort of story in which *Nancy's* career as a social worker comes into conflict with her marriage when she is offered an excellent job in her field—in California. Agnes sees *Frank* and *Nancy* as a very "now" couple, and feels this is the sort of conflict that might really happen to bright, contemporary young people like themselves. So *Nancy* and *Frank*, devoted to their marriage but also to their respective careers, will be torn by this situation.

Agnes comes up to New York in late September to discuss this as well as other long-range story developments with her writers, and also to watch auditions for "a new *Jeff*." Though *Mary* has been killed off and cannot be brought back later in the form of a new "reincarnated" actress, *Jeff* has only been sent off to work in a small clinic in Wisconsin, thus leaving open the possibility that he may sooner or later "return to Pine Valley."

This depends largely on when and if a suitable young actor can be found who must not so much be a physical likeness of the former *Jeff*, as an approximation of the image of what *Jeff Martin* of the story should look like according to Agnes' image of the character.

As well as searching for "the new *Jeff*" on that visit to New York, Agnes is anxious to watch the episode of the program that shows the final and dramatic departure of "the old *Jeff*," actor Charlie Frank. This particular show is to be aired on a Friday when Agnes has a luncheon engagement she is unable to break, and precludes her seeing the show at its regular air time, so she asks ABC to set up a screening of it for her the evening before.

I go with Agnes at seven o'clock that Thursday evening to the ABC headquarters building at 1330 Sixth Avenue, where Mike Brockman, vice-president of daytime programming, has arranged for the showing in a small, comfortable lounge across the hall from his own office.

Before the program is aired, Agnes explains that the filming of the final scene of *Jeff's departure* had been technically very difficult. It was one of the few outside shots the program has done, and a production crew with director and *Jeff* had been dispatched to a small cemetery in New Bedford, Connecticut, to shoot the scene. *Jeff* is to go to the cemetery where he will visit Mary's grave for the last time and place a bouquet of flowers at the site. The deceased *Mary* is to "appear" to him in a sort of translucent form, with the flowers and trees of the cemetery "showing through her," so that viewers will understand that this is a kind of vision of *Mary* or the spirit of *Mary* rather than her sudden return to the living (or the program). Agnes explains that since actress Susan Blanchard had already left—not this life, but the program—her part in the scene has been shot earlier in the studio and then superimposed on the cemetery scene where she "appears" to *Jeff*. One small but crucial part of this problem is to make sure *Jeff* looks at the "vision" of *Mary* where it appears, since in fact when he does his part she will not be at the scene in the cemetery.

None of this is noticeable when the scene is shown. *Mary* looks ethereal, *Jeff* seems reverently moved, and *Mary* tells him she won't appear to him any more but will always love him, that she wants him to live his life and carry on his work, for her sake, and then she de-materializes. *Jeff* rises from his kneeling position at the gravestone, tenderly leaves the flowers, stands, and walks slowly through the grass and trees, as the episode ends and the crawl of credits moves over his departing form, without the usual theme music but only a hush that is broken occasionally by the soft chirping of birds.

In the viewing lounge at ABC Agnes excuses herself, reaches for her pocketbook, and pulls out a handkerchief. She wipes at her eyes and apologizes for being sentimental about it, but she just can't help it. I say that's perfectly O.K. as I blink and brush my jacket sleeve over my eyes, as if to remove some foreign substance.

Mary and *Jeff* are now gone, and though *Jeff* may later return, Charlie Frank and Susan Blanchard are no longer part of the family. An era in the history of Pine Valley is over.

But at dinner, Fred Porcelli, the efficient maître d' of Pine Valley's Château Nick Davis and tonight of New York's "21" Club, takes us to our table, and after Agnes and I are fortified with a glass of Lillet, she tells me dry-eyed of new developments in the future of Pine Valley, some comforting, some shocking. She assures me that by next February *Anne Tyler* and *Paul Martin,* separated for so long, will be reunited and will "have most of their problems behind them." But new, unforeseen troubles are brewing. Had I noticed that handsome and mysterious new medical aide at the Pine Valley Hospital, the bearded *David Thornton?* Had I noticed how nurse *Ruth Martin* had taken at first a disliking to his rude manner, but now seems to becoming sympathetic toward him? Could I imagine that perhaps the faithful nurse *Ruth,* paragon of virtue, might in spite of herself, slowly but surely find after years of happy marriage to *Dr. Joe* that she is becoming interested in *another man?*

I order some wine, and promise not to breathe a word of it, or of the other surprising events that are being planned for the future of Pine Valley. I vow that, if anyone asks me, I will only answer with the advice I intend to follow myself:

Tune in tomorrow . . .

Act IV

FANS
AND FOES

Stephanie Braxton is appearing on a "Dialing for Dollars" television show in Philadelphia, before a live audience that includes a great many fans of "All My Children."

The fans are asking questions, and at first their questions are addressed to Stephanie Braxton, the actress who plays *Tara Martin Tyler*, the lovely young wife of *Dr. Chuck Tyler* and the former lover of *Chuck's* best friend, *Phil Brent*. The questions are about things like how did you get into acting, how do you like being on a soap opera, what is the daily schedule like. These questions are asked with interest, mildly, respectfully, and Stephanie answers in the same spirit.

Then a woman stands up and asks a question in a different tone of voice, a tone more urgent and aggressive than was heard in the other questions.

"Why do you insist on loving *Phil*," she asks, "when *Chuck* is so much nicer?"

There is a slight pause, and Stephanie smiles.

"Do affairs of the heart always make sense?" she responds. Now she is *Tara*.

The audience has finished questioning Stephanie, the actress, and now they want to interrogate *Tara,* the young wife from Pine Valley, and so Stephanie, smoothly and graciously, accepts the role and plays it. When the next woman wonders if she will ever leave *Chuck* and go back to *Phil,* Stephanie does not explain that she is not allowed to talk about future story developments; rather, *Tara* says wistfully, "I really don't know. . . . How can one ever know about such things?"

Another woman asks daringly, "What do you think about *Phil* going out with *Erica* now?"

In the story, *Tara* of course is jealous that her old love *Phil* is having an affair with the brazen hussy *Erica.* And so *Tara* answers, "*Well.* Of course I don't like it."

"Do you think," another fan asks anxiously, "that *Erica* is really in love with *Phil?*"

Tara answers huffily, "Well, of course *I* don't think so. Not *really* in love with him. . . ."

Stephanie is able to move back and forth across the shaky line that separates actor and role not only because she's a talented actress but also because the whole phenomenon of playing in a daily serial has a deep effect on the player as well as the audience. It is not like playing a part in a play that is the same every time and that you walk away from every night. This is the daily playing of the same character in a constantly *changing* part, a part in which you are doing different things and saying different things with different people, rather than doing and saying the same thing over and over with the same people, so that in a sense you do become more deeply identified with the part than an actor in a movie or a play. Stephanie explains it very well in another question-and-answer period, this time before a group of Ohio State University students, when someone asks her if she'd like to play another part in "All My Children," if she'd like to be one of the other characters rather than *Tara.*

Stephanie says, "That's very hard to answer. You become so involved with your character that it's like saying to you, 'Do you want to be somebody else, and if so, who and why?' And you could say, 'Oh sure, I'd like to be *Kitty* and independent,' or 'Sure, I'd like to be *Erica* and have all the men after me,' or

'Sure, I–' But it's like wishful thinking, because you become the thing–you begin to think of yourself in terms of your character, and about, oh, I'd say six months after being on the show–you can't imagine being anyone else. It takes about six months to become that involved."

And the involvement is deepened, like it or not, by the reaction of the fans, who seem to be everywhere. These are not the "closet" fans, the embarrassed intellectuals or culturally intimidated dowagers or macho-fearful men who don't want anyone to know they watch soap operas. These are the hard-core, unashamed, enthusiastic fans who stop you on the street and want to know what's going to happen next.

Bill Mooney, who plays lawyer *Paul Martin,* is telling me over a lunch-break omelet that "naturally, as an actor I'm grateful for the fans, but sometimes you feel it's a mixed blessing. The fans of the soaps have a different attitude than fans of movies or nighttime TV. Even if you're on a nighttime series the fans see you only once a week. But we're on every day, and the viewers feel they know more about you, personally, that they know *all* about you. They feel they have some kind of ownership of you.

"It's kind of spooky sometimes, even when it works in your favor. I wanted to buy some land in Colorado and the people selling the parcel I wanted were extra careful because it abutted their own land and they naturally wanted to sell to a person who'd be a good neighbor. The realtor told them I was *Paul* on 'All My Children,' and they watched the show a few weeks and decided to sell me the property. From watching *Paul Martin* they had decided that Bill Mooney was a real nice guy. I was pleased of course, but I couldn't help having this creepy feeling that if I'd been playing a villain they'd have never sold me the land."

When Ruth Warrick is on leave with the road company of *Irene, Phoebe* is supposedly on a "round-the-world cruise" and hasn't written home to her husband. Ruth writes to Agnes during this period that "*Phoebe* is being accosted on the streets by people saying, 'Please, send your husband a postcard!'"

Nick Benedict, who plays *Phil Brent*, goes home to visit his parents in Los Angeles during the time that, on the program, *Phil* is having a love affair with *Erica*. Nick is driving along Sunset Boulevard and as he pulls up at a stoplight the car next to him honks and the woman in it motions to him to roll down his window. The couple in the car are Sammy Davis, Jr., and his wife. Nick rolls down his window and Mrs. Davis shouts, "Don't marry *Erica!*" Sammy Davis, Jr., is nodding his head in emphatic agreement.

All right, we know that Sammy Davis, Jr., and his wife don't really think that guy in the car next to them on Sunset Boulevard is really *Phil Brent*, who has driven out to L.A. from Pine Valley while he ponders whether or not he should marry *Erica Kane*. But the illusion of it, and the confusion of the illusion with reality, is part of the fun of being a soap fan, and also part of the effect of following a daily serial. It *does* have a different effect on those who play in it and those who watch it than does a play or a movie.

Robert Redford is probably our biggest male movie star, right? But when he played the role of Jay Gatsby in the biggest extravaganza of the year, I don't think anyone pulled up next to his car and shouted, "Don't marry Daisy Buchanan!"

Fans not only tell the people of Pine Valley what they ought to do—who they should marry, how they should treat their mother, when they should get divorced—they also, if given the chance, ask them what they're *going* to do, try to find out what's going to happen next.

"Being on a soap," Fra Heflin tells me, "fans think they have a special claim on you. Most of them want you to tell them what's going to happen next and I say truthfully I don't know. That's one of the reasons I'm glad we don't get scripts far ahead of time and don't get to see long-term story projections. They come to you with all kinds of pleas, I mean *really*. I had one young man ask me what was going to happen to certain characters and he said he didn't want to know for his own sake, but his aged mother was dying, and might not live to know how this particular story was going to come out, and if only I would tell him it would make his mother's last days so much happier, and she could die in peace. Well, there are cases where you might be tempted to tell something that's going to happen, but you can't be tempted if you don't know. Thank God we don't know."

The few people who *do* know what's going to happen next are sworn to secrecy, and they are serious about it.

Bud Kloss won't even tell his own mother.

"Last Sunday my mother phoned me," Bud tells me, "and said all her friends wanted to know if *Phil* and *Erica* are going to get married. I asked her, 'And what did you say, Mother?' and she said, 'I said my son never tells me,' and I said, 'That's *right*, Mother, that's exactly what you should tell them.'"

An ABC public relations man drops in at Bud's booth one morning at McGlade's to ask Bud about a story request from a magazine.

"It's a publication called *Maturity*—something," the PR man says. "I can't remember the exact title, but it has 'maturity' in it, and I guess it's aimed at sort of a senior-citizen audience. They want to do a story on Hugh Franklin, asking him how he feels about playing the role of *Dr. Charles Tyler*, and how he feels about *Dr. Tyler* as a character, you know, as a model for older people."

"Well, that sounds fine," Bud says.

"But there's a hitch. They only want to do the story if, on the program, *Dr. Tyler* gets divorced from *Phoebe* and takes up with *Mona*. If that happens it will be a good story for them, you know, it will show older people they too can change their lives and find new romance. They think that'll make a real good story for their particular audience."

At this point in the program *Dr. Tyler* is threatening to leave his wife and take up with *Mona*, but it hasn't happened yet. Maybe it won't happen. Maybe he and *Phoebe* will have a reconciliation. Maybe . . .

Bud is shaking his head emphatically, and he slaps the table and says, "No. That's *our* good story, not theirs or anyone else's, and we won't tell them how it comes out till it comes out. I'll be happy to talk about any present or past situation and co-operate fully with publications that want to discuss those things, but I'll never talk about future story. That's the business *we're* in."

The fans may not be able to find out what's going to happen, even from buttonholing Bill Mooney while he's taking his kids to the amusement park, or by getting in good with Bud Kloss's mother, but of course they are free to write, as many do, and express their opinions about what *should* happen and what happened that they didn't like or did like and whatever else is on their mind.

Agnes says she and Bud read all the letters that are addressed to the show (many are addressed to the individual actors or "characters") and although they don't "tally them up" and do what most of the audience advises, Agnes says, "I learn a lot from the letters. I had always thought, for instance, that young people weren't interested in watching a story of older people's love problems. But there is a great deal of youthful interest in the *Phoebe-Charles-Mona* story. We get so many letters from college kids who are interested in that triangle, and most of them say, 'Please let *Mona* and *Charles* have an affair!'"

The letters to the cast are placed in a designated cubbyhole of a large gray metal mail rack on a table in the rehearsal room, and one day I ask Bill Mooney and Mary Fickett if I can look at some of their mail and they say fine.

Bill—or lawyer *Paul*—is told to stop being a fraud and start to think like a man before it's too late.

"When you get mad on the show, you sure are cute."

"As *Paul Martin*, you are the dumbest man I have ever seen."

A letter enclosing his astrology chart says, "Dear Bill, it must have taken a lifetime to make such a beautiful blend of planets. . . ."

Mary Fickett as nurse *Ruth Martin* has fans ranging from a fifteen-year-old girl who says, "I wish my mother was as understanding and loving as you are," to a young man about to enter the armed forces who says, "I would like to have you as my favorite pin-up girl."

A housewife asks her, "Do you like to cook? I like to bake. Do you have any good recipes that would be easy and economical for me to fix?"

In Bud's office I look through a pile of letters to the show, many of these urging certain courses of action:

"Please bring *Erica* out of the hospital and have *Dr. Tyler* divorce that bitchy wife."

But the "bitchy wife" has a supporter who writes, "I am thinking of making a profound change and not watching your show because the image of the mother *Phoebe Tyler* and the treatment shown her by her husband and children are not conducive to healthy, happy living."

Another fan complains that if *Mary* is killed off, "I'll stop watching the show! Several of my friends feel the same way!"

One critic asks, "Why is *Anne Tyler* always shown as Miss Innocent Victim of Circumstance when she is just as bad as *Erica* or *Margo* or anyone else?"

There is also some genuine appreciation:

"I like your show because it has humor and a few normal characters. The other soap operas are so gloomy and serious and glum all the time."

"I enjoy your show. Most soaps are all the same. They don't do anything different except change the person playing the part."

There are also letters to the show asking messages to be conveyed to the cast and/or characters:

"Tell *Margo* I like her face lift and tell *Phoebe* I like her hairdo."

"Tell Kay Campbell she is a real sweet person just like my grandmother is."

There are also pure testimonials, like this from a fan who writes, "I must say this show to me is like when one is hooked on drugs and can't give it up. Through this show I even turned down a better-paying job, for I was certain I could not have been able to watch 'All My Children.'"

Bob Greene, a correspondent of the Chicago *Sun-Times,* is trying to push his way through the crowd that is jamming the

Student Union Building on the campus of Northern Illinois University at De Kalb. He is there to do an article on the current mood of the campus, to find out what the hot issues are now among today's college students. When he finally makes his way into the main room, he sees the assembled throng is divided into two parts, each watching one of the two large color television sets at opposite ends of the room. Both sets are tuned to what appears to be a soap opera. Greene asks Joy Kampe, a senior at the university, what's going on.

"This is the biggest thing on campus," Miss Kampe tells him. "It is the issue the students are most concerned about."

Greene wonders how that can be; it seems to him the students are watching a soap opera.

"Not just any soap opera," Miss Kampe informs him. "This is 'All My Children.' There has never been anything like it around here. Students plan their class schedules around it. Right at this moment, 'All My Children' is on television sets in every fraternity, sorority, and dormitory on campus.

"'All My Children,'" she explains, "is supposed to be this big at colleges all over the country. It's what students want to see. I guarantee that two out of every three students on this campus—men and women both—can tell you the plot line of 'All My Children,' much more than could tell you the record of our football team."

There are similar scenes across the country. Another one is described by Fergus M. Bordewich, who writes in the New York *Times:*

"It's a gray afternoon in the Flatbush section of Brooklyn. The time is 1 P.M. A television set glowing dully across the room is tuned to 'All My Children,' a serial tale of frustrated young love among constantly distraught young adults. . . .

"The scene is the TV lounge at Brooklyn College. More than a hundred young faces—white, black, male, female—are staring fixedly at the television screen. All the chairs are filled. As still more students pack into the room, they squat on the floor or lean against the walls. And now, there's standing room only."

Bordewich reports that similar scenes are taking place in the dorms at Columbia, in the Loeb Student Center at New

York University, "in fraternity and sorority houses from Boston to Madison to Berkeley, in Ivy League college lounges and student apartments throughout the metropolitan New York area. . . ."

The cast and staff of "All My Children" get frequent requests to appear on college campuses, and whenever they can they do.

Bud Kloss goes down to the University of Miami, where a script of the show is performed in a drama class.

Larry Keith attends a banquet in his honor—or in *Nick Davis'* honor—at Williams College, and, in dashing *Nick Davis* style, flies up in his private plane for the occasion.

Mary Fickett gets a letter inviting her and her "TV family" to a testimonial dinner at Wheaton College in Massachusetts. The invitation says, "During our four years here we have come to realize the unique place 'All My Children' occupies in the day-to-day life of the college community."

Fra Heflin tells me that "my daughter is at Mount Holyoke and when I go to visit her on campus there's a minor revolution in getting to the dining room because *Mona Kane* is there. This really surprised me at first, the campus popularity, but it seems the young people are really into this show."

Agnes Nixon not only gets requests to appear before student fans or college classes but also to supply information for a growing number of graduate students who are doing dissertations either on soap operas in general or on "All My Children" in particular.

The campus craze over Pine Valley and its inhabitants is not just limited to colleges, either. The high school students are into it as well. The headmistress of the lower school of the Agnes Irwin School for Girls in Philadelphia asks Agnes if she'd come speak to the seniors at an assembly. The headmistress tells Agnes that "the girls have watched the show for four years—a year ago they did their class skit based on the show, and called it 'All My Juniors.'"

Agnes goes to the Irwin School assembly, and after telling them factually but informally about the production and writing of the show, she answers questions.

The first questioner wants to know if Susan Lucci is really like *Erica*—she just hates *Erica*—and Agnes assures her that Susan is a very sweet person, and then she asks, "You say you hate *Erica*, but don't you understand *Erica?*"

There is a deep, communal "Yeahhhhhhhh" from the audience.

"Because I've always felt," Agnes says, "that when I look at *Erica* I can say, 'There but for the grace of God go I, or my children.' It's understandable why *Erica* is the way she is, and we get mail that's sympathetic to her as well as hostile. That's gratifying to me, because it was my purpose that, since Susan Lucci is so beautiful, people can hate her but at the same time people who aren't so beautiful can say, 'She's that beautiful but she really isn't happy.' You know, the feeling that 'I've kind of got it made; I've got my head together better than *Erica.*'"

There are squeals and laughter and applause.

A student asks about the "older" love story, the triangle of *Dr. Charles Tyler,* his wife *Phoebe,* and his secretary *Mona.*

The student wants to know if *Mona* is having an affair with *Dr. Tyler* and Agnes says, "Well, not at this point, no," and the audience laughs delightedly, sensing they may have got a hint of what will happen.

Agnes says as if discussing the behavior of some neighbors with her own children, "I think *Mona's* just lonely, and *Dr. Tyler* is misunderstood by his wife *and* lonely, and right now they're having a very comfortable relationship."

Then Agnes leans forward, speaking in a more intimate tone, the tone of the storyteller drawing in her audience, pulling them into her confidence: "But *Phoebe* better watch out, hadn't she? If she keeps acting like this, she'll *push Dr. Tyler* and *Mona* together. That's what *I* think!"

Applause and cheers from the audience.

They are in the story now. Agnes has made them part of it.

Nor is this just "the children's hour" because it is in a prep school assembly. The same spirit and rapport with the audience, the same sense of storytelling takes place when Agnes goes the following month with Stephanie Braxton to Ohio

State, where they are the guests of the Drama Department and the Anthropology Department. Professor Henry Schwartz is using "All My Children" in an anthropology seminar because he feels that soap operas today both affect and reflect contemporary culture.

So of course there are serious questions about the meaning of it all, and, surprisingly, there are students asking about "How do you get into the business?" There are college students now who are interested in a career in soap opera!

And after a while there is the storytelling, though it starts from a more—sociological angle.

Agnes is asked why the men on the show aren't more aggressive, why the women seem to dominate everything. Agnes says she doesn't think this is always true, and as an example she brings up how *Dr. Charles Tyler* is finally revolting against his snobbish, nagging wife *Phoebe:* "It's taken five years, but *Charles* is finally telling *Phoebe* off. . . ."

Cheers and applause.

"You know," Agnes continues, "he's taken just so much and so finally he's moving out of the house and moving into his club—"

There is a hush, a sound of gasps coming from the audience, and Agnes says, "Oh! I don't know if that's happened on the air yet or not!"

There is laughter and applause and whistling and cheering.

The storyteller has, unwittingly or not, "revealed" a small part of what's coming next in the story. Agnes looks shocked, gasps, and says, "I told, I told!"

The fans are delighted. They know a little bit of what will happen next, enough to make them feel they're on the inside. But not enough to keep them from watching the story.

One Sunday afternoon a Princeton University student named Dave Kelley is at the Metropolitan Museum of Art and he sees a woman across the room who looks very familiar, but he can't place her. He tells a friend, "I know I've seen that

woman sometime recently and she was arguing with someone."

The woman is Mary Fickett and Kelley has seen her as
nurse *Ruth Martin* arguing with her husband *Dr. Joe Martin*
on "All My Children." When he realizes this he goes up to
Mary and asks if she and some others from the show will
come down to Princeton and speak before a seminar on popular culture he is in that is studying "All My Children."

Mary and Agnes and Bud Kloss and Susan Lucci go down
to Princeton and Agnes recalls the evening as one of her most
pleasant campus visits.

"It was a nice variety of students," she recalls. "Some of
them were fans who watched the show purely for entertainment, and others simply watched it because it was required
for the course. But all of them were bright and articulate. I remember one young woman complaining that we didn't have
the women in the program *doing* enough, and why didn't we
have a woman on the program run for Congress or something.
Well, before I could answer myself, another woman student
said that most women viewers probably couldn't identify with
a woman running for Congress, but they *could* identify with
Kitty Shea, who has gradually and meaningfully gained pride
and confidence in herself, has grown emotionally and intel-
lectually from a depressed female who let everyone walk all
over her, to an independent, aware kind of person. Of course,
I liked that because that's how I see *Kitty* myself. One of the
nice aspects of the evening was that the young man who
taught the seminar didn't let the students get too academic
about the whole thing. I remember, at one point, a student
launched into a long, overly symbolic analysis of the show,
and the teacher sort of gently cut it short, and said, 'Let's not
pull the butterfly apart. . . .'"

The teacher is a young historian named George Forgie, who
has a B.A. from Amherst College and a Ph.D. in intellectual
history from Stanford. His specialty is the nineteenth century
and he was teaching a lecture course at Princeton on "American Intellectual History from the Puritans to Ben Franklin"
when students began to ask for something more current and

popular. Forgie worked up a seminar in "American Popular Culture from World War II," ranging from *Peyton Place* to Norman Vincent Peale, and he figured he had the subject pretty well covered until a girl came in to apply for admission in the course, read the syllabus, and told Mr. Forgie he had left out the most important force in American popular culture, which was daytime television, and, more specifically, soap operas.

Forgie felt the point was valid but he'd never watched a soap opera, and he asked the girl which one the class should watch. She said there was no question about it, they should watch "All My Children." By chance Forgie had some friends in California—a man he had gone to graduate school with and his wife—who always talked about "All My Children" and made what were then to Forgie obscure references like "That's the sort of thing *Phoebe* would say," or "You're getting to be a regular *Nick Davis*." Forgie started watching the program, liked it a lot, and required the class to watch it on a regular basis.

"We started watching it by saying we'll examine the program to try to figure out why housewives watch it," Forgie tells me, and then he admits, "As we started getting hooked on it ourselves we got honest with each other and decided we'd better examine it to see why *we* liked to watch it.

"One thing we felt was appealing was that everyone likes to hear gossip, especially when they don't have to be responsible about it. And of course gossip is only interesting if it's about people you find interesting, and we really got fascinated with the characters *as people*. We liked the fact that *Erica* wasn't just a villain, she was both good and bad.

"Male and female students alike enjoyed it, and most of them were opposed to dissecting it too much. That seemed almost heartless, like analyzing the lives of your friends for a term paper. But we did analyze how the plot manipulated the people—the plotting is like a minuet, holding off inevitable confrontations and events, and then bringing them up center stage.

"We liked the humor, too. I find myself laughing out loud

sometimes watching it, the looks the characters give each other, the little nuances of the lines. Even when things are going badly for the characters, when difficulties are taking place, you don't feel they're doing Greek tragedy. You feel like the characters know what they're doing, like 'they're on your side.'

"I know 'All My Children' is cited as one of the more relevant soaps, dealing with issues like drugs and child abuse and so on, but frankly we didn't feel the 'relevance' was that big a deal, at least in why we liked it so much. We were more interested in when and how *Phil* was going to find out he was the natural father of *Tara's* child."

Forgie now teaches at the University of Texas at Austin and he says that "All My Children" is popular among the students there, too.

"I'm a Faculty Fellow for a girl's dormitory, and I was invited to lunch there a few weeks ago, and hardly anyone was in the dining room. I was told that most of the girls were upstairs watching 'All My Children'—it comes on at noon down here. I guess the best indication of how widespread a phenomenon it is among students was a squib in the student paper the other day, *The Daily Texan,* something about what would happen if *Phil* and *Erica* attended some student event coming up. The squib didn't even mention 'All My Children,' the paper just assumed that everyone knows who *Phil* and *Erica* are."

The History Department at Texas already has a "twentieth-century man" in intellectual history and Forgie has not yet devised a way of working "All My Children" into a course on the nineteenth century, but even though he isn't teaching the program now, he is watching every day.

"When I can't watch," he tells me, "I have a tape system set up that records when the show comes on. But I rigged the thing up myself and it doesn't always work. When that happens, I call this friend in California, the guy who I went to grad school with who's been watching the show almost from the start. He's writing his doctoral thesis on Henry Adams.

"Sometimes," he says rather wistfully, "I feel like it must be

an illness with me. I've got to have my fix every day. My in-
jection of 'All My Children.'"

"No, no," I assure him, "it's perfectly O.K. I feel the same
way. I'm just not ingenious enough to fix up the tape recorder
and all. We are fellow fans."

"Listen," he says, "you've been talking to Agnes, haven't
you?"

I say I have.

"Well, do you happen to know if this rumor going around is
true that *Chuck* is going to die?"

I say I don't know and anything I do know I can't tell, I am
pledged and sworn to secrecy. To change the subject I ask
him something I have wondered about his teaching "All My
Children" at Princeton, which is whether he was put down for
it, how his academic colleagues felt about it.

"I admit I was inhibited about telling people at Princeton I
was using it in a course," he says. "It was respectable to teach
and talk about popular culture, but I played down using the
soap opera. When faculty people asked me about teaching a
soap opera in my course I couldn't tell whether it was real interest or a kind of academic ridicule. I assumed there was a
general attitude of condescension about my teaching it.

"When I invited the people from 'All My Children' to come
down to Princeton for dinner and talk with the students, I was
nervous about asking my department for the money for that
purpose. So I didn't say the people coming were from a soap
opera. I just said, 'We have some guest speakers coming down
from New York.' And that was all right."

The soap stigma goes deep.

Agnes flies to Detroit to appear on "The Lou Gordon
Show," a syndicated television talk show that is going to ask
the question "Why are so doggone many women hooked on
soap opera," or, as he puts it another time, "Soap operas: are
they good or bad?"

On the "good" side we have Agnes; soap star George
Reinholt, then of "Another World" and soon to be on "One
Life to Live"; and Mrs. Bryna Laub, founder and publisher of
the "Daytime Serial Newsletter," which summarizes the plot

of each of the fourteen soaps during the past months for more
than 17,000 fans who subscribe either to keep themselves up
on any developments they may have missed or to savor the
story a second time by reading about what happened again,
or both.

The "baddie" stand is represented by Dr. Irene Kassorla,
described by the host as "a very famous psychologist who believes that daytime serials make mental cripples out of the
people who watch them." Dr. Kassorla is also the author of a
new book called *Putting It All Together.*

The Doctor—who at one point reminds the host that she is
indeed a doctor and should be addressed as "Doctor" rather
than as "Irene" (though George Reinholt says he doesn't accept the "pseudo-science" of psychology)—says she indeed
believes soaps are dangerous to the viewer.

As the three people who make a living in the world of soap
opera gasp and gurgle and fume, the Doctor emphasizes that
they are all right, they are fine people who obviously enjoy
their work and are good at it and are leading rewarding and
exciting lives.

It strikes me that there is some sort of contradiction here, if
the Doctor feels these people who create and publicize soap
operas are all terrific, but the thing they create and publicize
is frying the minds of millions of Americans; nevertheless, no
one picks up on that.

"*These* people are fine," she says, meaning Agnes and
George and Bryna. "I'm concerned about the housewife—she's
atrophying—she's shrinking up here and expanding down
there—she spends her life in front of the tube and it's *no fair*
to her."

The Doctor says the housewife comes out of high school all
eager and full of hope, and then "a few years out of high
school she's in front of that tube and she's almost without
hope. She's become a Peeping Tom."

And what malignant and mysterious force has deprived the
housewife of hope and turned her into a Peeping Tom?

Soap opera.

It's not television per se, you understand, it's soap opera.

Television could be a force for good, the Doctor explains, still speaking of the housewife:

"If she's going to be in front of the TV I'd like it to be something that could help her with her life, something that could be rewarding, fulfilling. If advertisers would provide her with something more meaningful than the soaps she'd watch that—she could learn to be more educated."

Learn to be more educated?

Of course.

The Doctor explains:

"They make 'Sesame Street' so exciting for the children in terms of education—I wish they could have an adult 'Sesame Street'—where housewives could learn maybe foreign languages, she could become more sophisticated."

Agnes says there are a lot of men and working women who watch "All My Children" on their lunch hour and she says, "The woman who takes her lunch hour to watch 'All My Children' is certainly going to object when you start teaching her Spanish."

The host asks the Doctor if she thinks women would really watch programs giving foreign-language instruction on television and she says emphatically, "Yes, if they made it more exciting for her."

The Doctor is now getting very excited herself, as she says, "They don't have to give her that senseless Mary-John-Matt-Lenore-Matt-Lenore-John-Mary-blah-blah-blah-blah-blah. . . ."

When it gets to the "Mary-John-Matt . . ." part, her voice turns angry and ugly, like a kid mocking his enemy with a series of "nyah-nyah-nyahs. . . ."

Bryna Laub says she doesn't think the Doctor has watched many soaps, not enough anyway to make these accusations, and the Doctor once again says it's not the terrific people here on the program she's attacking, but she does wish they could channel their energies into "something better."

Mrs. Laub points out how Agnes has written so many "public service" things into her shows, educating women, for instance, about the pap test, and getting many thousands of replies of appreciation, and how she now has worked in a story about child abuse and how mothers can get help in such a situation. . . .

The Doctor says that sounds fine but wants to know, "Why do they have to have all that other stuff." She evidently means the story.

The reason people watch.

After that program Agnes gets a number of letters from soap fans, one of whom holds the theory that the Doctor would like more people to go to her with their problems, but soap opera is "better medicine for me—and cheaper!"

Another fan indignant at the Doctor says, "If I were you I'd resent the whole bit—bitterly. An adult 'Sesame Street' indeed!"

But the Doctor is not the only critic who feels that soaps could better educate the viewers by the specific means of teaching a foreign language. The most ingenious suggestion I know is from Professor Rose K. Goldsen, a highly respected sociologist on the faculty of Cornell University, who has come up with the idea that soaps might simply be *spoken* in a foreign language. Professor Goldsen, in a commentary on the media on a local radio station in Ithaca, New York, expresses her concern over the influence of soaps on preschoolers. She tells her listeners, "If that stuff [soap operas] were broadcast in French, every child in the United States today would be a fluent French speaker. Yes, every child!"

If you ask me, the whole thing sounds downright un-American.

And speaking of being un-American, the soaps have been accused of that, too. While on the one hand critics attack daytime serials for not teaching foreign languages, on the other hand they have been attacked for allegedly aiding our foreign enemies! During World War II, a New York psychiatrist, Dr. Louis I. Berg, warned that the daytime radio serials were playing right into the hands of the Axis Powers, that Hitler & Co. wanted the American housewife to listen to soap operas, because they create a state of anxiety: ". . . the very same overanxiety which is the end of all enemy propaganda, for it lays the groundwork for civilian panic in emergencies and saps the productive energies of the afflicted individuals in all their essential efforts."

Dr. Berg, whose battle against the evils of soap is chronicled by Madeline Edmondson and David Rounds in their book *The Soaps,* also accused poor Ma Perkins and her pals of causing such a variety of dire symptoms as arrhythmia, tachycardia, vertigo, and high blood pressure.

Nor did Dr. Berg fling these charges around without first personally researching the matter. He chose some of the leading soaps of his time, including "A Woman in White," and, immediately after listening to the program tested his own blood pressure and found it rising! "A Woman in White" of course was created by Irna Phillips and was the first program Agnes Nixon worked on as a dialogist, so for all we know it might have been one of Agnes' own scripts that sent the first anti-soap psychiatrist's blood pressure soaring!

But since then, along with attacks and put-downs of soap opera from every sector of society, there has been at least a growing trickle of opinion from professionals that watching daytime serials may not after all be hazardous to your mental or physical health. In fact, there are some who think there might even be some advantage in it.

I hear from some friends who know that I'm writing a book about soap opera that there is a "soap opera therapy" group at Framingham Union Hospital, one of the most highly regarded hospitals in the Boston area, and I go to visit the therapist who conducts the group. Anne Kilguss, who is chief psychiatric social worker at Framingham Union Hospital, has written a carefully reasoned paper called "Using Soap Operas as a Therapeutic Tool" for a professional journal called *Social Casework,* and she gives me a copy as we sit in her living room and discuss how she came to be involved with using soap opera in her work.

"I got into soap opera through my patients," she says. "I was working at Boston State Hospital, and my patients were mainly black and lower-middle-class Jewish and Irish women. It was more of a working-class population. These women did not come from families where you talk openly about your feelings, and it was difficult for me to get them to talk about themselves. So I'd ask them what they did, and they'd say they watched soap operas. I said well, let's talk about them. I began to find they *would* talk about the programs, and then after a while they'd pick up themes that were problems in their own lives. They related to characters like themselves, who had similar kinds of problems."

As Miss Kilguss elaborated in her paper:

"When approaching such patients, I re-examine their lifestyles and values and recall the old adage of beginning where the patient is. If women watch soap operas, the discussion of such programs can open a path to the patient's unconscious and fantasy life. From the program, one works back to the individual and her concerns. This method may be comparable to using play therapy with children. Freud believed that dreams and jokes were the most direct route to the unconscious. I propose that the individual's use and interpretation of media is another. . . ."

Recognizing the importance of soap opera in the lives of her patients, Miss Kilguss took a three-week vacation during the summer of 1972, during which she picked out six different soap operas and watched them every day. Since then, she periodically takes a day to "review" them, to keep up to date on what's happening. In a profession that by and large dismisses soap operas out of hand, this is an unusual, if not to say courageous, path to take, and Miss Kilguss speaks frankly and critically in her paper of the prevailing attitude about such matters:

"After attending numerous case conferences and seminars, I postulate that social workers and their patients denigrate such contemporary phenomena as soap operas as being unworthy of discussion in the therapeutic situation. By such myopic professionalism, we are cutting off avenues to our patients."

The hospital where Miss Kilguss works now is in a suburb of more middle- and upper-middle-class residents than Boston State, but still most of the patients know the soaps and Miss

All Her Children

Kilguss uses discussions of them in group as well as individual therapy.

"Our soap opera therapy group is one of the most popular of any of the groups we have," she says. "People who like the soaps come to it, and others come who say, 'I hate soap operas, I can't stand them!' but they come anyway. My basic attempt is to bring the things they watch on soaps back to themselves, to get them to see how they behave and respond by what the characters do."

Miss Kilguss feels viewers use soaps in a number of different ways:

"Some are very sick people who watch soaps to learn new words, to learn how to get along with people. A lot of women watch who have kids, women whose husbands have left them, and they try to learn from them. Also, for women who are alone in the house with kids, it provides a chance to listen to adults converse with one another." And, as she points out in her paper, "For the individual who is constantly trying to keep up with a world he was not raised to understand, media offer advice on how to cope with this gap."

But all this does not mean Miss Kilguss endorses all of soap opera and thinks it's perfectly swell. She has a number of complaints and criticisms based on her own viewing of the programs. She feels that most of the characters "are not as complicated as most people. By and large they're portrayed as black and white.

"Also, I'd like to see more problem solving. Maybe they could show an amicable divorce; teach people that many who marry in their teens don't grow up until their middle twenties and for a couple like this who are having problems and have grown in different directions, divorce might possibly be a good thing.

"I'd like to see them show a woman whose kids have grown up and gone off to college. This is a dangerous time in a marriage, a turning point, and they might show how women work through it, how they find other ways to fill their lives when the children are gone.

"And I wish they'd portray how women feel losing their

looks, instead of all the soaps showing women at fifty who are doing fine and able to attract younger men. . . ."

I tell her about *Margo* having a face lift on "All My Children" in order to attract a younger man, and she admits "All My Children" was not one of the six shows she watched, and there may well be many things she didn't see that the other shows have dramatized.

I ask Miss Kilguss, if, in spite of her honest criticisms of the soaps, she enjoyed watching them, or whether it was purely a professional chore. She freely admits that "I find them very seductive, very entertaining."

I ask if, among those she watched and "reviews," she has a particular favorite.

Miss Kilguss hesitates, and then, with a somewhat sheepish but pleasant smile, she says, " 'Days of Our Lives.' "

I bet Miss Kilguss is a very good therapist.

After my talk with Miss Kilguss, as I am typing up my notes of our conversation, something strikes me that in all my reading and talks with people about soap opera is a recurrent theme.

Why do people expect so much of soap opera that they don't expect or ask for from any other medium of entertainment? Even as fair-minded an observer as Miss Kilguss wants to see the soaps do more to educate the viewers in areas of personal problem solving, in raising and dealing with realistic issues. Dr. Kassorla and Professor Goldsen want them to teach foreign languages.

Does anyone set such requirements for nighttime television, or even for Broadway plays, movies, and novels? I have never heard anyone attack "Mannix" or "Columbo" or "Kojak" for failing to teach their viewers how to speak French, nor do I know of anyone putting down "Mary Tyler Moore" or "Dick Van Dyke" for failing to come to grips with the painful social and psychological issues of our time. Did any critics pan *The Sting* for failing to upgrade the intelligence of its audience? Far from it, the movie was praised for what it sought to be, a

lively story, a good piece of entertainment, and was lavished
praise and showered with Academy Awards. *The Godfather*
was appreciated by critics and audience alike in a similar—
and I think suitable—manner as a fast-paced, well-acted, absorbing story. No one complained that the audience did not
come out of it speaking fluent Italian.

Yet soap operas, which are designed and aired and written
and acted primarily for purposes of entertainment, are attacked for not serving as a kind of combination night school
and therapy session, Berlitz course and consciousness-raising
medium, with a little of "Face the Nation," "Dear Abby," and
"Issues and Answers" thrown in.

The irony is that many—not all, but many—of the soap operas deal dramatically with more contemporary social issues
than any other medium of entertainment.

And, to compound the irony, when they do, they are usually
scorned for not doing enough of it.

"What Do the Soaps Have to Do to Win Your Approval?"

That is how the New York *Times* entertainment page
headlined a letter from Agnes Nixon in response to an article
by Terry Ann Knopf charging that "the soaps have yet to
come to grips with reality in any meaningful way."

It could no longer be charged that soaps fail to come to
grips with real issues of society, but it is of course always possible to claim that they don't do it enough or well enough.
Mrs. Nixon was particularly galled by Ms. Knopf's allegation
that "the subject of drugs has recently been introduced—but
is being handled with excessive caution."

Mrs. Nixon found this judgment perturbing because in its
own pages the New York *Times* had run a long and positive
article about how her serial "One Life to Live" had put one of
its young women cast members in the drug rehabilitation center Odyssey House and shot episodes on location with the actress and the young ex-addicts discussing their drug problems,
and these scenes were shown on the program throughout the
summer in an effort to educate young viewers who might not
read newspapers or watch documentaries about the dangers
of experimenting with drugs.

Of all daytime serial creator-writers Mrs. Nixon has the most right to feel frustrated by charges that the soaps don't "come to grips with reality in any meaningful way."

Mrs. Nixon refers to just some of the many issues she has dealt with on her own programs in an article, "In Daytime TV, the Golden Age Is Now," in the *Journal of the Academy of Television Arts and Sciences:*

"We have done the story of a young college couple living together without benefit of clergy. We had the first legal abortion on television. We have dealt dramatically with the subject of male infertility. . . .

"A five-month campaign to inform women of the efficacy of the pap smear test in detecting uterine cancer in its early stages brought a bonanza of mail from appreciative women across the country. . . .

"For almost two years we told the story of a young Negro woman of light pigmentation who passed as white. This sequence was done primarily because it furnished us with an intense, absorbing drama that attracted viewers. But the mail response substantiated our belief that it was absorbing *because* it was relevant and because it explained to viewers the sociological motivations for such a denial of heritage and race, due to the rejections suffered by the young woman from both the black and white communities. The ultimate tragedy we were presenting was simply another instance of man's cruelty to man, instigated by ignorance and prejudice. . . .

"We have had an eight-month campaign to educate viewers —particularly the young ones—to the endemic proportions of venereal disease and all its ramifications. We followed this with an article on the subject—supposedly written by a young reporter on the program—which we offered to any viewer who requested it. 'Venereal Disease: A Fact We Must Face and Fight' also gave the address of the Venereal Disease Branch of the Public Health Service for Disease Control in Atlanta, Georgia, for anyone wishing to get further information on setting up some type of educational program in his (or her) own community.

"Over 10,000 requests for the article were received by ABC

and, according to William Schwartz, educational consultant
for the Public Health Bureau, letters arrived at his desk from
all over the country in a steady stream, all as a result of the
story and the printed piece. To quote Mr. Schwartz, 'We were
never before able to reach, effectively, the teen-agers who are
most in need of this information but you have shown us how
it can be done.'"

Other subjects Mrs. Nixon's serials have dealt with include
ecology, mental health ("particularly the very common anx-
iety-depression syndrome"), the danger of carbon monoxide
poisoning in the home, the problems of readjustment of a returned POW, a soldier missing in action in Vietnam, a woman
peace activist, and problems of child abuse and how troubled
parents trapped in such a pattern could get help.

And remember, all this was not done on a series of PBS
documentaries. All this was done as an integrated part of a
continuing story on two five-day-a-week daytime serials. Soap
operas.

Mrs. Nixon is surely justified in asking, "What do the soaps
have to do to win your approval?"

One sometimes reaches the conclusion that in fact there is
nothing the soaps can do to win the approval of many of their
vehement opponents. Agnes could put John Gielgud on "All
My Children" playing King Lear for the Pine Valley High
School drama class, she could have Bill Buckley debate
Arthur Schlesinger, Jr., at the Pine Valley Country Club on
the perils of world Communism, she could have Allen Gins-
berg recite "Howl" on a poetry night at the Château Nick
Davis, let Julia Child give lessons in French cuisine to
Grandma *Kate Martin,* get Thurgood Marshall to argue the
issue of urban busing with lawyer *Paul Martin,* have a Chi-
nese physician teach acupuncture to *Dr. Charles Tyler,* have
the idealistic young *Phil Brent* join a United Nations team
that goes to Africa to aid starving children and shoot scenes
on location in the slums of Uganda . . . and still I doubt very
seriously that her program could win the approval of the
critics. Why not? Because it's called a soap opera. Period.

I find the anti-soap attitude summed up most purely at a

party given by a friend in Boston when an attractive and intelligent young woman psychologist comes up to me and says she hears I am writing a book about a soap opera and wants to know, "How can you?" She says she simply can't stand soap operas, she thinks they are all absolutely terrible. I ask why she is so down on them and she says she supposes it's because women come to her with *real* problems, and so she resents the fact that so many women watch soap operas and soap operas only gloss over real problems, no one on soap operas ever really suffers or feels any real pain. I say this is rather ironic because one of the big criticisms of soap operas is that the characters suffer too much, that they just have one problem after another, and critics say real life isn't like that. I ask the psychologist which soap operas she has watched that have given her the impression she has just expressed, and she says she has never really watched any one soap opera for the full half-hour program because "after five minutes of watching one I get so nervous I just can't stand it and I have to turn it off."

Soap opera is one of the few media that critics don't have to watch in order to feel justified in despising.

It's little wonder that people who work in soap opera don't use that denigrated term except when they're talking to outsiders, who don't know it by any other name. But when "soap opera" actors or directors or production people are talking among themselves they call the medium they work in "Daytime Serials" or "Daytime Television" or just "Daytime," as in "I work in Daytime," or "I've been in Daytime for fifteen years," or "I first went to Daytime in 1960."

The soap opera stigma is washing off now a little—but slowly.

Judith Barcroft admits that "when I started acting in soaps I was embarrassed to say I did soap opera—then they started getting better actors, even famous actors. I think it's a lot more 'in' to watch soaps now. I get a lot more intelligent letters than I got five years ago. I used to get mainly scrawls, but now a lot of the letters are typed, and they're not just asking me as *Anne Tyler* to do this or that, to leave So-and-so and take up with So-and-so. A lot of these letters are very thoughtful.

"But still the old cliché survives—that it's all a joke. For instance, when any of us go on a talk show, they introduce us by playing that corny old organ music, and everyone giggles."

Charlie Frank says acting on a soap "does have a kind of stigma. You spend all that time training, and then it comes down to a choice between artsy-craftsy or legitimate theater on the one hand, and commercial theater on the other, and commercial theater includes the soaps. The first couple of years out of school, your old classmates say, 'How can you do soaps?' And then later they say, 'Gee, you think I could get on a soap?'"

Del Hughes, one of the two directors of "All My Children," directed one of TV's first soaps, "The Brighter Day." He quit in 1959 to do theater work and then when he tried to get back in television found his soap experience a handicap:

"When I went to discuss directing jobs with TV networks and producers and they'd ask what I'd done on TV and I'd mention soaps, I could see the door close. I could see it immediately happen. But I don't think soap's a dirty word any more, at least among professionals. They're slowly starting to recognize the kind of work we do and the caliber of the actors."

When Ginny Payne, the original Ma Perkins, and Kay Campbell, who once played Ma's daughter Effie and now is *Kate Martin* on "All My Children," talk with me over lunch about their years in soap opera, Ginny says, "You know, they used to talk about 'silent drinkers,' the ones you never heard about, and I think in that same sense there's an awful lot of 'silent viewers' of soap operas."

Kay agrees and says, "But I think it's changing now. The attitude toward serials. It's an idea whose time has come. Ginny, did you see the wonderful article on soap operas last week in *The New York Times Magazine?* You've got to get it. It's a real breakthrough. It talks about how professors and college students watch the programs, and how they're being taught in college courses. After all these years it's finally happening. We're getting respectable!"

I think Kay is right in her appraisal of the *Times Magazine* article as "a real breakthrough." Written by former Washington *Post* foreign correspondent Anthony Astrachan, the article, called "Life Can Be Beautiful/Relevant," is the most thorough, informative, and fair-minded journalistic account of the soaps I have read. Mr. Astrachan wrote that the "clinching evidence" of the appeal of soaps comes in figures, and he states them succinctly, accurately, irrefutably:

"There are 14 soaps now on the air, watched each weekday by 20 million people. Although each soap has been half an hour long since 1956, 'Another World' recently expanded to an hour and 'Days of Our Lives' will follow suit next month—possibly initiating a trend the others will follow. The average program has 6.7 million viewers according to the A. C. Nielsen research organization, and the number is growing as recession keeps more and more people at home. More than 11 per cent of the viewers are men. The households break down economically and educationally in proportions similar to the population as a whole—51.4 per cent with household incomes under $10,000, for instance, and 23.9 per cent with incomes over $15,000. About 24.8 per cent of household heads have only an elementary school education, while 56.2 per cent have a high school education or better. The 14 serials cost more than $50-million a year to produce; actors make a minimum of $211 per half-hour show and go up to a maximum of $100,000 a year, while a writer makes a minimum of $310 a show, and a good head writer makes $3,000 a week after paying his subwriters. The programs gross more than $300-million a year from the makers of soaps, deodorants, cake mixes and other household products, providing a disproportionate share of network profits though nighttime budgets are much larger."

The article appeared in the New York *Times Magazine* issue of March 23, 1975, and within the next seventeen days I note that there are four articles on soap opera in national magazines, Agnes Nixon appears on a panel discussion devoted to soap opera on "The Tomorrow TV Show," and on

the "Today Show" Barbara Walters "discovers" a soap opera
that has been "right down the hall from us for thirteen years,"
and drops in on these newly recognized neighbors to chat
with them about the sort of work they do.

Mrs. Bryna Laub, founder and publisher of the increasingly
popular "Daytime Serial Newsletter," writes in an editorial a
few months after the Astrachan article that soap opera might
be in for a "renaissance":

"For all too long there existed a smirking aspect to references about 'soap opera.' Indeed this very term, coined dec-
ades ago in reference to the corporations which sponsored the
radio prototypes of today's dramas, had often been maligned
in the hands of some professional critics . . . to denote syrupy
content in films and books. However, today, there is a growing acceptance that 'soap opera' denotes a particular type of
drama—one which shows character growth and development
in a continuous format. This category rightly includes such
prime-time presentations as BBC's 'Upstairs, Downstairs' and
'The Waltons.' I wonder had these programs been shown at 2
p.m. instead of prime time their reception would have been as
quick or their acclaim so universal. Some prejudices die hard."

Indeed. Especially the soap stigma.

TV Guide writer Edith Efron is amazed to learn that a male
friend of hers who is a distinguished economics professor at
NYU is also an avid soap watcher, and she goes on to discover
many males are hooked and writes an article on the phenomenon for her magazine. When she tells the economist about all
the different types of men she discovered who watch soaps he
says, "Oh, there's been a big cover-up going on. I think a lot
more men watch than *say* they watch. But so many other
things are coming out of the closet these days—why not intellectuals watching soaps?"

But when Ms. Efron asks him then if she can use his name
in her article he says, "Good heavens no," and says it would
be "disastrous."

Nor is it only a stigma for men. Intelligent women are not
supposed to watch soaps, either. Beth Gutcheon, author of the
book *Abortion: A Woman's Guide,* writes an appreciative ap-

praisal of soaps for *Ms.*, but admits that "the fact that you're watching soaps isn't the sort of thing you want to get around."

Ms. Gutcheon concludes the stigma comes because "I think the people are not contemptuous of the serial form, nor of the content, but of the audience. Women. Women who stay home. Women who 'don't work.' Housewives."

My own opinion is that the soap haters are contemptuous of *both* the audience and the form and content of the serial dramas. The cliché housewife soap watcher is never seen as an intelligent, active, educated woman who may take time out from her duties and interests to watch one or two soaps during the day (the average watcher), but rather she is seen as the dim-witted dunce in the tacky housecoat glued to the tube all day long.

But I also believe there is contempt for "soap operas" as a form, a contempt going back to radio days when in fact the programs were far less sophisticated and far more open to the kind of attack James Thurber made in his definition of soap opera that is still, though outdated, the standard appraisal today. Thurber wrote that soap opera is "a kind of sandwich, whose recipe is simple enough, although it took years to compound. Between thick slices of advertising, spread twelve minutes of dialogue, add predicament, villainy, and female suffering in equal measure, throw in a dash of nobility, sprinkle with tears, season with organ music, cover with a rich announcer sauce, and serve five times a week."

Less noted or even known is the judgment of the respected critic of popular culture Gilbert Seldes, who in his book *The Great Audience* called daytime serials radio's "single notable contribution to the art of fiction." He praised the way the serial had adjusted itself to the listening patterns of housewives and had developed a "technique of narration as skillful as that of Joseph Conrad, and, in its way, as complex."

The most time-honored method of putting down the soaps is to state the plot over a period of time, and the bare plot always sounds silly. Take for instance, the description of the following plot:

". . . the story verges on melodrama when it isn't pure fairy tale; a rich uncle, a poor niece, an ugly sick cousin who worships her from a distance, three suitors, a fairy-godfather who converts the niece into an heiress, and finally her betrayal by a couple of her cosmopolite compatriots into a marriage as sinister as the backdrop of a Brontë novel: of such time-worn threads is this woven. . . ."

Certainly sounds trite and silly, doesn't it?

That is the plot of *Portrait of a Lady* by Henry James, as described by the great James biographer Leon Edel, in his introduction to a paperback reprint of the novel. Mr. Edel after summarizing the plot adds that it is a true description, "and yet to say this is to offer a gross caricature of a warm and human work."

The stating of a plot is inevitably a gross caricature, as James himself well understood. Edel tells us that James felt "that the story itself is not necessarily what gives a novel its life; that the writer can invoke the implausible in certain circumstances and render it plausible; it was the *way* in which the story was told, the qualities of mind and heart that flowed into it, suffusing it with the warmth and texture of life itself, that made it real to the imagination of the reader, whose mind and experience in turn play over the recorded experience. Thus many of the grotesqueries of Dickens flame into reality for us, and the fustian of Dostoevski and the eeriness of Emily Brontë."

The same point can be made about a continuing story seen on television, where again it is not the story itself that gives it life but the way it is told—and in this case also the way it is acted, directed, and produced.

People who work in soap opera always cite Charles Dickens as their ancestor, and though the scoffers pooh-pooh the idea, as distinguished a literary critic as Northrop Frye feels the daytime serials are "Dickens-derived."

As a writer of serials—and all his fifteen novels first appeared in serial installments, at either monthly or weekly intervals—Dickens in fact faced many of the problems of the current daily TV dramatic writer, and solved them often in similar ways. The problem of recapitulation that the TV serial writers and actors find so annoying and so necessary was also a burden for Dickens.

In a study entitled *Dickens as a Serial Novelist*, Archibald Coolidge points out:

"The problem of the reader needing to know where he was and where this or that detail fitted was very pressing. It was pressing not only at the beginning of the novel but again and again at points during the novel when new installments began and the reader might have forgotten or confused this or that pattern during the month-long intervals before."

We tend to forget that the great nineteenth-century novelists—and great they were—were in their own time ordinary mortals worrying about the bills to pay and the critics' complaints, working against deadlines, plotting around the end and beginning of installments. We forget such scenes as that of Anthony Trollope sitting up late into the night with a towel around his head as he finished an installment of *The Way We Live Now* to give to a waiting messenger boy to take to the press.

Henry James, the Master himself, wrote some of his finest novels serially—for the express purpose of making more money to live on so he could write more novels—and was not above changing his story in response to the opinions of the audience. When *The Bostonians* was appearing in installments in *The Atlantic Monthly*, there was an angry outcry from readers who felt his portrayal of the suffragette character Miss Birdseye was too harsh, and so the author in ensuing installments softened and changed her to a more sympathetic character.

The fans of the nineteenth-century serials were just as rabid as those of today—there was no TV then and these were *their* continuing stories. Historian Henry Bragdon recalls being told by his Great-aunt Melissa when she was ninety-three how she remembered ringing the bell for the farmhands to come in from the fields when the latest installment of *Uncle Tom's Cabin* arrived and how they all gathered round and the eldest son of the family read the installment and then everyone returned to their labors.

Biographer Edgar Johnson, in *Dickens: His Tragedy and Triumph*, writes that when Dickens' *The Old Curiosity Shop* was being sent to America in shipments of the latest install-ment, "waiting crowds at a New York pier shouted to an in-coming vessel, 'Is "Little Nell" dead?'"

Our own judgment is so clouded by the stigma of soap that it is unfair even to look at the TV serials and make any histor-ical critical or artistic judgment of them, but it would be fas-cinating if future generations of scholars and critics could see them and discuss their value and their contribution to their time, just as we now look back on the serial works of the great nineteenth-century novelists.

But these hypothetical future critics will not have the op-portunity to make such judgments and comparisons. For unlike the novels of Dickens and his contemporaries, the tapes of most of the television serials will not exist. In fact, most of those that have been aired are already gone. The networks de-stroy them, because they don't want to "waste the space" that would be necessary to store them.

The most popular stories of our time will never be seen again.

Act V

HOME

The "Bible" or presentation Agnes wrote for "All My Children" does not begin with a description of the characters or the outline of plots and subplots that will be developed, but rather it opens by describing the locale, the imaginary setting of the story, the place where it all will happen.

"The community of Pine Valley is almost as important in our story as are the characters themselves. A settlement whose roots go deep into pre-Revolutionary soil, the Valley has a distinctive personality and charm which affects all who live in or near it. And though it is a self-contained community, its role of suburb to a large eastern city, as well as its proximity to New York, makes it unique from most small towns or suburbs in other sections of the country.

"Pine Valley has a very fine community-supported hospital, an excellent fire department and police force, one high school, three elementary schools, and a healthy variety of churches, synagogues and meeting houses.

"Although there will be other characters, major and minor, our story, its plots and subplots, will deal primarily with two families in Pine Valley: the Tylers and the Martins. . . . Not all the members of these families live in Pine Valley, nor will the stories concerning them always take place there, for we shall not be confined to one locale. Yet the Valley will be what everyone thinks of when they think of 'home.' Home because, whether living there or not, this verdant Valley has, in some way, made them what they are and is, to some extent, part of them."

From watching the program for four years, I feel very much aware of Pine Valley as a place—and yet, I realize I have never actually seen it on the screen. Before reading Agnes' presentation for "All My Children," all I really knew about Pine Valley geographically was that it is an hour's train ride from New York City, and a long airplane flight from Seattle.

I know these things because when the citizens of Pine Valley go anywhere, they most often go to either New York or Seattle. *Erica Kane* went to New York to get an abortion and, later, a job as a model; *Phil Brent* went there to stop *Erica* from having another abortion when she was pregnant with his child; *Margo* went there to have a face lift; *Tara* went there with other Pine Valley residents for a day-long cultural tour of art museums; *Nick Davis* went there to hear some night-club acts to see if any might be suitable to perform in his supper club in Pine Valley. As I recount these New York excursions, it strikes me that New York City is to Pine Valley residents what it is to most of the rest of us who live outside of it. Like the Pine Valley residents, most of us other outlanders are happy when we have completed our business there and get to come back home.

When Pine Valley people don't take the hour journey to New York, they most often seem to go to Seattle. When *Lincoln Tyler* left Pine Valley he went to practice law in Seattle. When *Anne Tyler* wanted to recover from her traumatic divorce from *Paul Martin* she went to Seattle for several months to stay with her brother *Lincoln*. Sometimes *Phoebe Tyler* goes to Seattle to visit friends.

I ask Agnes why Seattle is such a favorite city among the people of Pine Valley and she says, "Well, you know, it's far away. Pine Valley is only an hour or so from New York, so we know if they go to Seattle they're really going on a long trip and will really be far from home."

I accept that of course, but I think there may be some other reasons. Residents of Pine Valley could also go far from home

by traveling to Los Angeles or San Francisco. But it is hard to
imagine Pine Valley people going to either of those places,
unless of course *Erica Kane Brent* takes off to Hollywood
someday on a mad, impetuous, and clearly self-destructive im-
pulse to try to get in the movies. Los Angeles, or at least its
national image among people who don't live there, is a cor-
rupt and sinful place bereft of the very values embodied in
the history and spirit and, as Agnes says, the very "soil" of
Pine Valley.

As for San Francisco, our national consciousness does not
evaluate it as evil but rather, and this is a kind of respectable
cousin of that concept—sophisticated. Some of the Pine Valley
residents are certainly sophisticated—that is, in knowing the
social graces and the amenities of fine wining and dining; of
appreciating, as *Lincoln Tyler* for instance appreciates, con-
certs and classical music. But sophisticated as *Lincoln* and his
sister *Anne* and his parents *Charles* and *Phoebe* may be, they
are not sophisticated in what most of us conceive to be a San
Francisco kind of sophistication. To me that implies a special
sort of pretension. Oh, I can imagine certain situations in
which some Pine Valley residents *might* go to San Francisco. I
can imagine that *Phoebe Tyler* might go there on some kind
of cultural-social weekend sponsored by her country club, or
maybe *Tara* would go there if she won a free weekend trip to
San Francisco on a game show with all expenses paid, but I
am sure that after a couple of cable-car rides she would want
to leave early and get back to her son, *Little Phillip*.

No, Los Angeles and San Francisco don't seem right for
Pine Valley people, but if they do have to leave town for a
while Seattle indeed seems perfect.

The national image of Seattle, at least as I read and hear
about it from friends (some of whom have gone to live there),
is that of a quiet city which has great physical beauty and a
lot of rain. But Seattle rain is not believed to be punishing as
in "a hard rain's gonna fall," or in the slashing, palm-bending
rains that come to Los Angeles every winter in a month of wet
fury; Seattle rain is a soft rain, a gentle rain, and then after it's
over, a mild and mellow sun comes out and the people of

Seattle go for walks. Seattle is not a place that is thought of as a center for people who want to "make it," in terms of either money or fame or sophistication. It's a place where people go who are tired of those races, or never wanted to be in them in the first place. I have never been to Seattle; of course, I am giving the national mythology about it that I have absorbed over the years. I picture the people there going for their walks, smiling, seeing the reflection of their smiles in the puddles on the streets and sidewalks. People from Pine Valley would be comfortable in Seattle. . . .

The small-town setting is of course nothing new in soap opera, and has occasioned many of the put-downs of soaps for being a fantasy world set most often in, as one recent critic put it, "Anytown, U.S.A." The history and rationale of the small-town settings are more thoughtfully described by Raymond W. Stedman in his book *The Serials*, when he notes that beginning with the radio soaps:

"Some of the day-time serial cities were real ones—Chicago or New York or Los Angeles. But small or middle-sized communities with imaginary names were far more prevalent. Serial writers created the communities of Hartville ('Just Plain Bill'), Elmwood ('Pepper Young's Family'), Three Oaks ('Young Dr. Malone'), Henderson ('Search for Tomorrow'), and many more.

"The locations of these fictional communities were left to the imagination, although the general-American dialects and occasional references to changes of season suggested that the towns lay somewhere between Illinois and New York. Nothing, however, prevented a listener from placing the communities wherever she wished to. Rushville Center could be right down the road if a housewife fancied it that way. And if she wished to believe that Elmwood was just another name for her own home town, then Pepper Young and his family might be just around the corner. It was not difficult to find at least one imaginary town that seemed a lot like home."

And this is part of the appeal of course, the providing of a place, if only fictional, that seems like "home," a place that for growing numbers of rootless or urbanized Americans doesn't exist any more. As Wisner Washam puts it:

"I think the Pine Valleys still exist, and the show appeals to people who live there, and maybe more importantly to people who used to live in some place like it and have left and still miss it."

Anne Kilguss, the psychiatric social worker who runs the "soap opera therapy group" at Framingham Union Hospital in Massachusetts, believes that one of the appeals of soaps "has to do with the breakup of the extended family, and the isolation that comes as a result of that. Women with very young children living alone with them—children two and three years old—watch soaps to have a peer group, to have company, by watching the lives and listening to the conversation of people their own age—it's like having a circle of friends. And older ladies, alone now, watch to have families they can relate to. You can watch the soaps over a period of years, and get to know the people on them better than your own neighbors, and with greater intensity."

In the absence of "real" homes and families, and often in big cities a lack of "neighbors" whom you know and speak to, the daytime television serial can provide at least a fictional substitute. In a mobile and constantly shifting society, often without roots or ties, a serial like "All My Children" is something to hold on to, to depend on, and I think that is one of its appeals to collegians, as expressed by the student spokesman of a delegation of seniors from Duke University who visited Agnes to express their appreciation of the program and tell her, "The show is one of the few constants in our lives."

I think the viewers also find appeal in the sense of values they find in Pine Valley, values that are generally felt to be too old-fashioned or square or irrelevant to be discussed in contemporary movies or "serious" fiction. I mean, for instance, how residents of Pine Valley, even the young ones, talk about family loyalty and the importance of "roots." When young *Phil Brent* is laid off his job with the Environmental Protection Agency in Pine Valley and then is offered a position in their Dallas, Texas, office he can't imagine leaving Pine Valley. The principal reasons of course are that he is still in love with *Tara* and he wants to be near his natural son and hers, *Little Phillip,* but even aside from those factors he explains to his mother he can't conceive of leaving Pine Valley, because "my *roots* are here."

Kitty Shea wants to try to find her mother even though her mother abandoned her as a child, and explains to *Lincoln Tyler,* "I guess you always love your mother, no matter what."

Lincoln smiles and says a person like *Kitty* always does, meaning a good person, a sensitive person, a person of character.

In between the traumas and trials of contemporary life, which are portrayed with emotional and social credibility in Pine Valley, there are also respites, those "Tea before the Telegram" sort of interludes I described in my introduction, and in Pine Valley these occasions usually emphasize the sense of family, of home, of roots, and how those elements are sources of nourishment.

Lawyer *Paul Martin,* after storming out of his apartment following a scene with his bitchy stepdaughter *Claudette* and his neurotic wife *Margo,* goes to get away from it all, not to a local bar, but back home to his mother's house, the home of *Kate Martin.* It's a warm sunny day in spring and they sit out on the white wooden frame porch of *Kate's* house and *Paul* loosens his tie and says how he enjoys this place, how he has such pleasant memories, like when he and his brother *Joe* when they were boys used to sit there and try to spit watermelon seeds over the railings, and *Kate* remembers how they made gallons of homemade ice cream. When *Paul* says he hasn't had a bite to eat all day but he doesn't want to put *Kate* to any trouble she naturally assures him it's no trouble at all and comes back out with a big plate of lunch and *Paul* pronounces the potato salad the best he's had since he left home. His mother says she doesn't know which of her roses to enter in the garden show this year, the red or the yellow; and the thought of yellow roses brings back to *Paul* the memory of his first wife, *Anne,* with whom he is still in love, and so we are back to the complexities and problems of lawyer *Paul's* existence. But there was the rest and respite, provided not by booze or drugs but by home and mother, memories and potato salad. . . .

Such scenes are worked in naturally, as part of the fabric of the place, along with the sophistication and the traumas of modern life, but it is important to know that these touches are done gracefully, and are not only nostalgic but fictionally credible. I think it's important to emphasize that Pine Valley is not one of those corn-ball, cracker-barrel, pseudo-folksy pipe-dream places such as we have seen presented in night-time viewing, most obnoxiously (to me anyway) in "Apple's Way," with George Apple, supposedly a contemporary man who is seeking his roots by going back to Iowa and living in a converted mill with his wife and kids and good old Grandpa, all of them aw-gee-in' and shucks-in' along like a bunch of castoffs from the down-home commercial where Euell Gibbons slurps his Grape-Nuts.

Only in nighttime television, supposedly for "adult" viewing, can they get away with that pap. I seriously doubt that a daytime audience would swallow it. They are accustomed to contemporary patterns of speech and thought, and the spectacle of a bunch of grown-ups gee-whizzing and golly-sakes-alive-ing around an old converted mill while they sought the good life and anguished over whether to risk their life savings in hopes of rescuing the town paper because they feel a community needs a locally owned paper, is part of what a community is all about, part of the values the rosy-cheeked Apples were trying to find when they moved back here to the land—well, shucks-a-Friday, you can get a better and more believable story than that by tuning in to any daytime serial from "As the World Turns," one of the oldest, to "The Young and the Restless," one of the newest.

Pine Valley is as up-to-date as it is possible to be for a story that is conceived and plotted as much as six months ahead of time, scripts written about a month in advance, and performances taped at least seven days ahead of being aired. Sometimes the writers and staff are trapped, as when they had *Phil Brent* get drafted to go to Vietnam and after the show was taped the draft ended. They have to be careful, so when they speak of contemporary issues it is something like, as Henry Kaplan put it looking at a script one day, "We're very big on inflation this week." Something that is going to be around for a while. And the characters do make comments on the larger world outside to show they know what's going on. My favorite such "contemporary" observation came from nurse *Ruth Martin*, who, when told about some kids brought into the emergency room of the Pine Valley Hospital, injured in an automobile crash because they were drinking, shakes her head and says, "These kids—first it was drugs, now it's alcohol."

The people of Pine Valley are up-to-date, if not on the latest headlines, on the general customs and attitudes and concerns of contemporary life. Almost everyone has cocktails before dinner, and some imbibe a fine wine at one of the local gourmet restaurants. There are abortions and divorces, mental hospitals and shock treatment, drugs and betrayal, wars and unemployment, just like in our "real" world. But there is also the feeling that somehow behind all that, propping up and providing a floor for the people of Pine Valley, are these big solid pillars of tradition, and behind them, protected by them, a huge vat of Grandma *Kate's* vegetable soup that will ease all sorrows, cure all ills. And that is one of the deep appeals of the place.

Talking about the show, Wisner Washam says he wishes they could do more exteriors, actually "show" Pine Valley, but budget restrictions prevent it. I say in a way I'm glad I never have literally seen it, since I have a conception of it in my imagination and I don't want to be disappointed, as I'm sure I would be, by seeing actual streets and buildings of a particular town. I think it would be something like the disappointment I felt on first seeing "The Lone Ranger" on television after I had pictured him so satisfactorily just by hearing him on the radio in the years I was growing up.

The production restrictions are severe, when you think this whole multi-family drama is shown with a limit of four different sets each day—that is, you can have the *Martin* Living Room, the Boutique, the Château Nick Davis, and a room at the Hospital. That's it. The next day you can switch and mix around, but on no day can you use more than four sets, for the simple reason that there isn't room for more in the studio. The budget also restricts the use of many more actors than the principal ones under contract.

Judith Barcroft says, "That's why Pine Valley looks like it's been hit by the Plague—there's hardly anyone around in stores or restaurants because it costs to hire extras. I used to complain and say, 'As long as I own this Boutique, why can't I have some customers?'"

The restriction to interiors and the restriction of the number of sets also result in other little oddities about Pine Valley.

Bud Kloss says, "People kid me and say Pine Valley is the only town they know that is made up entirely of restaurants. So much of our action takes place in restaurants because we have to have someplace inside for people to talk, in addition to private homes, so we have people talking to each other over lunch or dinner or drinks or a cup of coffee in some restaurant. I've been told that restaurants must be the principal industry of Pine Valley."

If restaurants are the principal industry, the Hospital is the main institution of Pine Valley and again for practical reasons. Agnes explains to students at Ohio State that "you have to understand we are within the walls of a studio and limited to four sets. A hospital is our equivalent of the old marketplace. It's a grand place to meet people, much better than the supermarket, it helps us to avoid having to employ the long arm of coincidence all the time. But we still have to do it quite a bit, I know. I mean, I blush sometimes when we have someone say, 'Well, I was *just* passing by, and so I stopped . . .'—you know. But how else does one do it?"

With all the restrictions, they do it quite beautifully. Within the four walls of the studio, with only the four sets to work with, they somehow convey the impression of Pine Valley being "home."

Ruth Warrick writes Agnes Nixon from one of the cities on her tour with the national company of *Irene* that "it will be good to be home again—in my own apartment, and on 'All My Children.'"

The sense of "home" and "family" is felt not only in the fictional Pine Valley but also among the people who create it.

When Agnes and Bob's production company, Creative Horizons, Inc., sells the show to ABC, Agnes writes a letter that goes to each member of the cast, telling them, "I shall remain with the show, furnishing the writing package, and this is merely to assure you of the continuity of our successful operation."

She expresses her appreciation to them, saying, "There is simply no way for me to truly express—shameful admission for a writer though it be—what our big little show, and you who are such a vital part if it, have meant to me over the past five years and will continue to mean.

"In spite of all our inevitable problems and traumas, there is a bond reaching past friendship into something mystically familial which enriches beyond measure. I can't help but think you feel it too, since it suffuses the screen so often. . . ."

The "familial" part is obvious and understood, the "mystical" part is a little more unusual. It has to do in some way with how some of the actors feel that what Agnes writes for the characters they play sometimes comes true. Like Charlie and Susan falling in love as their characters did, and Charlie feeling, "Agnes is writing my life for me." Like Judith Barcroft being hesitant about her son Ian playing *Little Phillip* when the child in the program is supposed to fall from a treehouse and have to be in the hospital and have an operation. Judith is afraid Ian might get sick if she lets him play it, but Agnes points out that *Little Phillip* won't be in the hospital because of an illness but because of an accident in a treehouse, and after all there aren't any treehouses around where the Washams live on Riverside Drive in Manhattan. Judith agrees, but in fact the day she is to take Ian to the studio he does get sick, not seriously, but a stomachache, enough to prevent him from going, and it is only because Ian pleads to go again that Judith finally consents, and happily everything turns out all right. Someone on the program got pregnant after Agnes wrote her character getting pregnant, and the woman felt that had something to do with it. Agnes' daughter Emily urges her mother to talk more about these occurrences of life mimicking the script, but Agnes firmly says, "No, I don't want to talk about it. All I'll say is some of the cast do feel that what happens in the script has affected their personal lives. That's all I can say. I don't want to be known as the Witch of Bryn Mawr!"

Charlie Frank, in addition to falling in love with Susan, his stage lover, has also formed a warm bond of friendship with Ray MacDonnell, who plays *Dr. Joe Martin*, his stage father. And both he and Susan are social friends of John Danelle and Lisa Wilkinson, who in the show are *Dr. Frank Grant* and his wife *Nancy*, who are the best friends in Pine Valley of *Dr. Jeff Martin* and his wife *Mary*, who are Charlie Frank and Susan Blanchard. . . .

Fra Heflin, who plays *Mona Kane*, the mother of *Erica*, is a close friend of Susan Lucci, who plays *Erica*. This older and younger woman share a dressing room together at the studio, and after Susan has her child, Fra spends all her free time knitting a sweater for the baby. When Susan comes home from the hospital, Fra throws a shower for her, attended by Kay Campbell/Grandma *Kate*, Mary Fickett/*Ruth Martin*, and Agnes, who comes up from Bryn Mawr for the occasion.

Nick Benedict, who plays *Phil Brent*, tells a TV fan magazine interviewer he "adores" Mary Fickett, who plays his mother, *Ruth Martin*, and in fact calls her "Mom" because he feels she's like a second mother to him, and he's learned a tremendous amount about acting from her.

If not everyone shares outside relationships that match their Pine Valley relationships, there is a general feeling of friendship and camaraderie, the sort of thing Larry Keith expressed when he told me, "I could pick up a telephone and call anyone on this show and ask for help, and I'd get it."

Peter White, who did *Barefoot in the Park* on Broadway and *The Boys in the Band*, and who plays *Lincoln Tyler*, tells me that:

"Before coming on this show I'd done two soaps, and I had

vowed never to do another. But this came along, and I liked
the part, and more importantly I liked the people involved, I
liked the atmosphere.

"I worked on one soap where you weren't allowed to smoke
or eat in the rehearsal rooms. The director ran it like an army
camp. You had to learn the script word for word, you couldn't
change anything, you couldn't make any suggestions. As you
can see, this is entirely different. Even with the inevitable
pressure, people are relaxed here. They feel at home."

Wisner Washam says, "Socially, we see a lot of Mary
Fickett, Bill Mooney, and Eileen Letchworth. There's a family
feeling among the cast, and also, beyond that, among the people from other soaps and the people on the fan magazines, the
whole 'industry' of the soap world. We had our baby daughter's christening last July, and we invited friends from 'All My
Children' and also from other shows, as well as some of the TV
fan magazine people—writers and photographers and editors.
The magazine people love those kinds of occasions—it gives
them a chance to see people from different shows all at once,
and in an informal setting. And it's nice for us, too. It gives
the illusion of something like our own version of the old
Hollywood, where everyone knew everyone and felt a common bond by being in the same industry—but instead of
Hollywood and the movie people, it's New York and the soap
people."

Milburn Smith, editor of *Afternoon TV*, tells me how he
personally enjoys the social as well as the business aspects of
daytime television:

"This is a very friendly world—there's a family feeling
about it—for one thing all of us who are in it are stuck with
the burden of the 'soap opera' label. If someone says a Broadway play is 'soap opera,' that's of course a put-down. This is a
label we're still fighting over."

The feeling of being a beset minority, branded with the
lowly "soap" label, indeed is part of the feeling of banding together against the outside world. As Agnes describes an aspect of this in her article "In Daytime TV, the Golden Age Is
Now":

"If we're unappreciated, you may ask, why do we work so hard in daytime TV? What drives us?

"That our jobs pay well is surely part of the answer. But it is not the basic one. Moreover, our salaries are meager alongside the prevailing nighttime scale. No, some other factor must account for the amazing esprit of these companies. I believe it is the pride and stimulation that comes of performing well in the face of all our restrictions and handicaps.

"Aside from ability, our work requires a stamina, a tenacity and self-discipline of which many people—even talented people—are incapable. Thus a sense of elitism, as intense as it is idiosyncratic, sustains us. (After all, if the Roman gladiators could have it, why not we?)"

Elitism. Yes. There is a phenomenon that we might call the "reverse stigma" in the soap world, so that just as people with soap experience are sometimes scorned by the outside world of theater, movies, and nighttime TV, so veterans of *those* media are sometimes spurned by the soapers.

Gordon Russell, who was groomed by Agnes to be head writer for "One Life to Live," tells me how it took him four years to break into writing for soap operas.

"Although I started as a playwright I'd mainly made a living writing for nighttime television, and when I went around to interview for jobs with daytime shows, they'd seem to be impressed with my credits and then they'd say, 'Have you ever done daytime?' and when I said no, that would be it. No job. Finally a head writer gave me a chance—he gave me an outline of a script to dialogue, I took it out of my typewriter and handed it to him and he read it and hired me. I've been in the business ever since."

Gladiators. Discipline. Yes.

During my lunch with those two gracious gladiators of soap opera dating from the early days in radio, Ginny Payne and Kay Campbell, who played together as Ma Perkins and her daughter Effie, the subject of discipline comes up. It arises because I ask naïvely why in all the photographs of scenes of radio soap opera stars in the studio, they are always *standing* around the microphone. I wonder why they didn't sit down around a table, whether that wouldn't have been more comfortable than standing up, and since no one could see them, why did they have to stand?

Ginny and Kay look at me and look at each other in a way that makes me feel I have missed some terribly obvious point that everyone with any sense at all ought to know.

"Discipline," Ginny says firmly. "We had discipline."

"Exactly," Kay agrees. "And maybe there was something about your voice sounding better if you stood up, but mainly I think it was discipline. Oh, we had discipline all right. Did you ever hear anyone hiccup on a daytime radio show? Or cough? Or sneeze? No, sir. We had discipline."

They also had their own world of radio soap opera actors and workers and sponsors, a world of mutual respect for craft and talent. And in that world Ginny Payne was a major star, for, as Ma Perkins, she was probably one of the most popular performers in radio, and therefore of course one of the most valuable.

Kay says, "Oh, if you'd only known the parties they gave for Ginny. Procter and Gamble gave these parties for her, every year—the most beautiful parties. At the Plaza, the St. Regis, the Racquet Club. . . ."

Ginny says softly, "I don't think they do that any more."

"Oh," Kay goes on, "there were all those courses—there was terrapin, grouse . . ."

"There were gold invitations," Ginny says.

There was also the camaraderie.

"Most of us on 'Ma Perkins' were from Chicago," Ginny recalls, "and we were a clannish group, especially when we first came to New York. It was a unique atmosphere on the 'Ma Perkins' show—there was very little individual competition. We were a group."

Kay Campbell, who now is Grandma *Kate* on "All My Children," tells Ginny with enthusiasm, "We have that same sort of spirit on 'All My Children'—this is the *happiest* show I've worked on in television. It's the closest thing I've known to the spirit of the 'Ma Perkins' show."

It's hard to be happy at eight in the morning.

Outside the rehearsal room in a sort of waiting-room area Bill Mooney, Charlie Frank, and John Danelle are reading *The New York Times* and drinking coffee. I say hello, they greet me, and Bill yawns and says, "I hope you can tell us why people watch these things."

That's how it feels at eight in the morning on a miserable cold March day.

Inside the rehearsal room someone has forgotten a line for the second time and says, "I guess I better write it down, huh?"

Del Hughes, who's directing today, puts down his script and tells about an actress he knew on another soap who wrote lines on the scenery, and the cameramen had to be careful not to pick up the writing.

Ray MacDonnell says he remembers that woman, she was on "All My Children" for a few days.

"She planted big pieces of paper all over the place with lines on them. They were scattered around like *leaves*."

Mary Fickett says, "We did that once on a Christmas show. You know, whenever there's a show where everyone wants to get home early, everything goes wrong and everyone forgets their lines. Well, we had pieces of paper with key phrases printed on them planted all over the place."

After the second run-through Del goes downstairs and discusses with Felicia Behr, the associate producer, what to do about an upcoming scene in a sequence on child abuse in which they need to have a child crying.

Del says, "If we can just get the kid in the bed and get him crying for a minute—and tape it right then—without scaring the kid in any way, that's what I'd like. But we'll have to talk the whole thing over with the parents, of course. Maybe we could get the mother to do something that would scare him *just a little* and then she could reassure him. His mother should be right there."

A cameraman comes over and says, "Maybe we could give him a lollipop and then take it away from him. Then if he cried we could tape him, and as soon as we finished the tape we could give him back the lollipop."

Del is sighing.

Mary Fickett comes off the set to use the phone. She says her daughter is home with the flu and she's been trying to reach the doctor but can't. Mary asks Felicia, if the doctor calls and Mary's on the set, would Felicia please ask the doctor to visit her daughter, then call Mary back and say what's wrong and what medication she should get.

I go out on the floor with my pencil and notebook, taking down notes about what different people are doing, and the stage manager comes up and politely introduces himself and asks if I mind telling him what I'm doing.

I tell him I'm a writer and I'm writing about the show and a big smile of relief comes over his face and he shouts to the rest of the crew, "It's O.K., boys, he's just a writer."

I ask what he thought I was, and he says, "The boys were afraid you were an efficiency expert. You know, sent by management or something to make a report on how we work."

I assure him I'm just a writer, and everything's O.K. now.

Back in the control room John Danelle is fuming over an article in one of the fan magazines about Francesca James.

"They have this headline, see, 'Francesca James Loves to Be Admired by Men.' Actually, what it was, they asked her what she thought about women's lib and she said she believed in equality and all that but she still liked a man to open a door for her. I know 'Chi Chi,' we went to drama school together at Carnegie Tech. In this article they made her sound like—well, like something she isn't. Some of them love to get these big juicy headlines, you know, so it makes it sound like we're all some kind of high livers. Wow."

Bill Mooney asks if I'd like to go across to McGlade's for something to eat, and I say fine.

When Bill takes off his coat in McGlade's he pulls from his pocket what seems to be an ordinary mustard bottle, one of those plastic jobs that most hamburger joints have that you squeeze the mustard from. I wonder if Bill has some dietary problem that requires him to carry his own special mustard around with him, and he smiles and says, "Just watch, I'm going to have some fun with this."

Bud Kloss is coming in and Bill says, "Oh, Bud—" and stands up, holding the mustard container, and says, "I'm having some kind of trouble with this thing—" and aiming it right at Bud's clean white shirt, Bill squeezes the container and a thin yellow stream shoots out and Bud yelps and jumps back and for a split second I wonder if reasonable, down-to-earth lawyer *Paul Martin* is actually played by some erratic crazy who squirts mustard on the clean white shirt of the Producer! I think for a moment Bud is wondering if Mooney has flipped, as Bud swipes his hand madly at his shirtfront, but it is still clean and then we both see Mooney standing there grinning as the apparent "stream of mustard" hangs limply and harmlessly out of the container, a yellow string.

"Oh," says Bud with relief. "Where in the world did you get that thing?"

"A joke shop," Bill says. "And don't worry, I'm not turning into a prankster. I needed some props for my e. e. cummings show, and this is something I'm going to use."

Bill tells me over an omelet and a Coke that he is doing a one-man show of "e. e. cummings' works" that Henry Kaplan is directing.

"I figure with the popularity of 'All My Children' in colleges I might as well try to make some raids on the campus."

He is also planning to do a play with Larry Keith that a playwright friend of theirs is working on now.

In addition to their "All My Children" work many of the cast members are involved in outside theater productions as well as commercials. Right now Peter White is rehearsing a new James Kirkwood play, and Judy Barcroft is understudy for Trish VanDevere in an O'Neill play soon to open.

Bill Mooney does a Burger King commercial; Larry Keith does the toothpaste commercial that shows the kids' cavities when they brush with some red ointment, and he also does a number of "voice-overs"; Charlie Frank does wine, English muffins, and shaving cream; Susan Blanchard does No-Nonsense panty hose. . . .

After lunch Judy Barcroft is told by Felicia to call her agent, and after the call Judy drops into a chair and says Trish VanDevere is sick and she's supposed to come to the play rehearsal tonight and they're putting her on salary right away.

"The play opens in three days," she says.

She picks up her script for today's show and starts going over lines, her mouth moving silently.

A loudspeaker is calling: "All My Children—Red Chairs; All My Children—Red Chairs."

This is the session when the director gives his "Notes," and it is called "Red Chairs" because the actors sit around squeezed behind one of the sets on these red canvas chairs.

Del Hughes is telling Ray MacDonnell during "Chairs" that he keeps saying "proneness" instead of "accident prone" and Ray says, "I know—I'm saying it because it's less awkward than saying 'because of his having been accident prone.' It's more natural to refer to his 'proneness' to accidents."

Del says it may be more natural but there's no such word as "proneness."

Ray says there *is* such a word.

Del asks if it's in the dictionary.

Ray says if there's a dictionary he'll find it and he goes off in search of one.

Del goes back to the control room to find that the bell on *Mona's* door on the set is broken.

A technician suggests, "You can't get hurt with a door knocker. We've got plenty of door knockers."

Mary gets hold of her daughter on the phone, and is trying to find out what the doctor told her.

"No, darling, I can't guess how much money you have. Listen, darling, I'm sure you have more than I do." *Ruth* is being called on the loudspeaker and Mary says firmly now, "Darling, I can't guess any more, I'm on the *set*."

Ray comes in with a dictionary and shows Del the word "proneness."

A sound technician tries different rings for *Mona's* doorbell. One is judged too loud and one too soft.

Sherrell Hoffman, the production assistant, says, "Split it down the middle."

Felicia nods and says, "Yeah, that sounds like *Mona's* bell."

"If we can't tell the difference, who can?" Sherrell asks.

"Are you kidding?" Felicia says. "Just wait for all the letters we'll get that say, 'That wasn't *Mona's* bell! Whose bell was that? What happened to *Mona's* bell?'"

Now Del discovers there are fingerprints all over *Mona's* door.

"What a mess," he says. "Who's in charge of that?"

Someone says it will be taken care of right away.

Del sighs, taps his pencil, and says to Sherrell, "And where will *you* spend eternity?"

Sherrell, not missing a beat, says, "*This* is eternity."

That's what it feels like sometimes.

One of the family is getting married.

This is a "real life" marriage for Ruth Warrick, but already some of the fans have confused it with the character she plays, *Phoebe Tyler*. In the story at this time *Phoebe* has returned to Pine Valley from her "round-the-world cruise" and is having marital troubles with her husband, *Dr. Charles Tyler*.

There have been items in the press about Ruth's impending wedding to Mr. Jarvis Cushing, including a long account of the forthcoming proceedings in "Suzy's" column in the New York *Daily News,* and Ruth stops Bud Kloss in the hall and says, "Do you know, I'm getting letters from people warning I'd better not marry this Cushing man until I divorce *Dr. Tyler!* They say I can get in a lot of legal trouble!"

It's a busy day in the studio for Ruth, she is having to make some calls about last-minute wedding arrangements, and in addition to her regular performance she has to do a "post-taping" of a scene with her serial son *Lincoln* so she can have an extra day off after the wedding. As she promised Agnes, she is *not* taking a honeymoon, but by doing this taping of one scene after the show she can have a day off.

The only time Ruth has free to talk with me is while she's having her hair fixed, so I follow her into the mirror-walled makeup room where Judi Morrison, the show's hair stylist, will shape and trim her hair. Ruth gets into one of the big barber-style chairs and I pull up a small aluminum chair beside it and put my notebook on my knee, alternately glancing up at Ruth and looking back down to record what she is telling me.

"You know that before and after dress rehearsal we have what we call 'Director's Notes' or 'Red Chairs,' and the director tells us what we're doing wrong, how we can improve, we all discuss what's working and not working. Sometimes the 'Chairs' are like a psychiatrist's couch or a confessional—there are things we share with each other that we wouldn't discuss anywhere else. We all respond to each other, and feel safe in telling each other our problems. It's a personal as well as a professional relationship.

"I think one thing that makes this so much nicer than the other soaps I've been on is Agnes and all the people who run it—they aren't 'show biz' types. They are people who have families, people who have values, standards—they are people of character, and of—of *breeding.*"

Ruth suddenly stops, looks up at Judi, and says, "Oh my God, I'm sounding just like *Phoebe* now! But it's true, isn't it, dear?"

Judi agrees, and says that as well as the things Ruth mentioned this is an *intelligent* group of people.

Ruth says that while she was happy to get back home to "All My Children" after being in the cast of *Irene,* she had to get adjusted to getting to bed early so she could get up early and "in the first few days I was in sheer terror of how I was going to remember all those lines.

"The other thing was, I really am affected by the emotions of the story, and there I was coming home to all that trouble—my own children, *Lincoln* and *Anne,* were in conflict with me, and husband *Charles* was obviously involved with that—that *Mona Kane* woman. . . ."

From my left, in the next chair, comes the voice of Fra

Heflin, who plays *Mona Kane,* saying very steadily and coolly, "Let's not lay too heavy on that—*Mona's* a lovely lady."

Ruth/*Phoebe* jumps slightly, looks around, and says, "Why, Fra, of course, darling!"

I feel as if I'm eavesdropping on two rival ladies who have met accidentally in the beauty shop while one caught the other putting her down.

Ruth/*Phoebe* says to me emphatically, "Of course, Fra and I are dear friends. Why, I'm friends with her whole family. It's so amusing, when people see the two of us in public they really freak out, thinking we're like *Phoebe* and *Mona.* But no, really, *Mona* is a lovely character, a lovely kind of woman."

Fra/*Mona* says, "That's a little better."

Ruth/*Phoebe* goes on to explain to me, "Anyway, even though *Mona's* a lovely woman and all that, I certainly don't want to do as *Charles* is asking me to do and go apologize to *Mona.* Why should I apologize? What on earth *for?*"

Fra/*Mona* says, "Oh, for heaven sakes, what does it matter? *Charles* really loves you anyway, regardless of what else is going on. You're the one he loves."

Ruth/*Phoebe:* "Oh no, my dear, he finally admits he's in love with *you.*"

Fra/*Mona* rises out of her chair. "You're kidding!" she says with true disbelief and dismay.

Ruth/*Phoebe,* sounding rather smug now, says, "Oh no. He loves you, and he's finally going to admit it."

Fra/*Mona,* still erect in her barber chair, says, "How do you know that?"

A pause. Ruth/*Phoebe* examines her fingernails. "I saw the script," she says.

Fra/*Mona:* "When?"

Ruth/*Phoebe:* "I can't remember, dear. All I remember is that *Charles* finally admits he loves you."

Fra/*Mona* falls back in her chair with a deep sigh and says, "Oh, Jesus Christ."

Judi asks Ruth to come to another chair down the line for some different type of work, and we pass by Fra/*Mona,* who is sitting in silence, her eyes closed, and when Ruth gets up in the new chair she tells me, "I do have to be careful not to let the *Phoebe* emotions affect my real life. I have to be careful that it doesn't carry over. When I get too sharp with my soon-to-be husband he says, 'Watch out, that's *Phoebe* coming out,' and I recognize it and stop. Now when I leave the studio, I try to have a moment of meditation, and say to myself, '*Phoebe*, you are gone now; this is Ruth.'

"But I do feel the emotions of *Phoebe* on the set. When I came home from that cruise and found that my own family had invited *Mona Kane* to Christmas dinner. My daughter *Anne* told me this and when she left she slammed the door but even though I was terribly angry at her I was also terribly hurt and as soon as that door slammed I really fell apart. In playing scenes with people screaming and yelling you really get caught up in it, and at that moment I said, 'Oh God—' and then in a flash I remembered we can't say 'God' except as a prayer, and I thought I had ruined the scene and we'd have to retape but then after just a slight pause I said, '. . . help me,' so it came out, 'God help me,' and you see, that made it a prayer!"

Ruth has to get in costume and I thank her for the talk, and go to sit back in the control room to wait and see the taping. There is technical trouble. One of the microphones that runs from the control room to the earphones of the cameramen is making a terrible shriek. Technicians are trying to find the cause.

Felicia Behr, the associate producer, is there with a stack of papers, and she can't concentrate anyway because of the shriek and I tell her Ruth's story about making a swear into a prayer and she says, "Oh yes, that's a big problem. We're allowed only so many 'hells' and 'damns' if it's an especially fraught situation. I've tried to get us an 'oh shit' a couple of times, but nothing doing. And 'God,' as Ruth told you, can only be used in a reverent manner."

The day is longer because of the post-taping of the scene with *Phoebe*, but before that Bud passes the word around that there will be a surprise party for Ruth in the makeup room, and everyone is invited for a brief champagne toast.

There are champagne bottles and small plastic cups and most of the day's cast members squeeze into the makeup room and everyone cheers when Ruth comes in and Ruth is given a glass and someone makes a toast to her, "May this one be the last!"

Ruth recalls the toast wishing the honored person money and fame and happiness *and* the time to enjoy it and she says, "And I always want to add, 'and the *strength* to enjoy it!'"

There is laughter, and Larry Keith says, "You're right, Ruth, we've all got the time, what we need is the strength."

Bud Kloss proposes a sincere no-frills toast for "Love and Happiness," and everyone drinks this in the respectful spirit it is offered and Ruth says, "Thank you."

Eileen Letchworth makes a toast, saying, "May the happiest day of your life so far be the unhappiest day of your life from now on."

There is some murmuring, and director Henry Kaplan says, "I'm not sure I *get* that."

"It sounds kind of Oriental," Bud says.

Ruth spots me, raises her glass, and says, "You see what I told you earlier about these people, how it's a family! It's true."

I raise my glass.

Ruth's wedding guests include her own family, her husband's family, friends of both, and members of the "All My Children" family. Representing Pine Valley are Agnes and Bob Nixon, Mary Fickett and her husband Leonard Sheer, Judith Barcroft and Wisner Washam, Kay Campbell, and Henry Kaplan.

Ruth is gracious enough to invite me so I can see this "extension" of Pine Valley family life, and I get a ride up with the Nixons and the Washams.

It is a cold, crisp day in late March, and Bob Nixon drives us up the Hudson River and into Connecticut. We pull up to the grand house on the hill overlooking silver-brilliant water, and Judy Barcroft says, "I'm so relieved—the house is just the way I thought it would be—the way I wanted it to be."

The maids who take our coats are giggling with excitement as they see the people from Pine Valley. They address Judy as *Anne* and ask if her brother is coming. Judy says no, but—and she figures quickly in her mind—and tells them nurse *Ruth Martin* will be here, and Grandma *Kate*. They are pleased and all aflutter.

The ceremony takes place in a beautiful glassed-in sun porch off the living room, and trumpet and piano music heralds the entry of the attendants and the bride and groom. The minister says we are gathered here to honor not only those we love now but those we loved in the past and those we will love in the future.

It is a quietly happy occasion, and after the ceremony the trumpet and piano music is replaced by that of two electric guitars. They are playing "Sweet Gypsy Rose," and I hear someone sing along of "rings on her fingers and bells on her toes." The men and women are of all ages, in finery of all kinds, from formal to informal; there are tuxes and velvet suits and corduroys and plaid wool jackets, and glittering gowns and colorful dresses. A light snow has started to fall, like a decoration, sprinkled over the water and sky, and there is a twenties quality about it all, not wild but nostalgic, pleasant and light and pretty.

Agnes is talking with Ruth and some of her relatives and a photographer comes up and Agnes starts to move away. Ruth pulls her back, saying, "You *have* to be in it. You're the 'Mother of the Bride'!"

BEAUTY SHOT

Agnes is driving me to a place near her home in Bryn Mawr that is special to her. It is a small historic church whose cornerstone was laid in 1775, St. David's of Radnor. It is an Episcopal church, founded by Welshmen, and though Agnes and her family are Roman Catholics, she has a personal love for this church and its particular kind of beauty.

"It's very simple and plain," she says, "like I think all churches ought to be. And it's open all the time, all hours of the day and night."

We go in the doors as another couple goes out. The day is one of intermittent rain and shadings of mist and fog, and we are the only people here now. Each step echoes on the bare wood floors. There is a small choir loft, and a simple white altar, backed by a large window. There is a hushed and restful silence.

I feel as if I have been here before, and I realize I have seen this room, or one very like it, and it comes to me that I have seen it on "All My Children." I ask Agnes if this isn't like the church where *Phil* and *Tara* stopped in a snowstorm and exchanged their own personal marriage vows before he had to leave the next day for Vietnam and there was no time to have a formal or even legal ceremony.

"Yes," Agnes says, "I thought of them having that marriage

here, not only because I love the church, the way it looks, the simplicity and the history of it, but also because it was possible—because St. David's is open all the time, *Phil* and *Tara* really *could* have come right in here out of a snowstorm and had their private ceremony."

We go into a small adjoining room which has many mementos of the church's history, including the original handwritten poem that Longfellow was moved to write after visiting St. David's during the American Centennial of 1876. The poem was "Old St. David's at Radnor" and he gave the manuscript of it to the church. This place where we are standing now moved Longfellow to write:

> Were I a pilgrim in search of peace,
>   Were I a pastor of Holy Church,
> More than a Bishop's diocese
>   Should I prize this place of rest and release,
> From further longing and further search. . . .

Even now, another and infinitely noisier centennial later, there is no sound of horns or jets as we stand here, no clatter or confusion, no clanging and buzzing of the instruments that make up such a part of the clamor of our daily lives. There is only the sound of our steps on the plain wood floor, and, when we stop, as we do, because it is a place to stop and appreciate the temporary cessation of all the grinding and screeching machinery of modern life, we hear nothing but the sound of our own breathing. It is both a surprise and a comfort, hearing that breathing that is the only sound in the midst of the otherwise unusual stillness. It reminds me I am alive. Most often that seemingly simple perception is drowned out in the chaos of our clangorous existence. We are alive here. We can hear it.

We pause for a while, agnostic and Catholic, man and woman of very different styles of life, not looking at one another, but sharing the almost silence. I think, though there are no words, or perhaps because of their absence, this moment can appropriately be called a kind of prayer.

I cough, and walk to a small desk where there are postcards

picturing the church and I take one and put a coin in the donation box. The description on the card says there are historic figures buried in the cemetery ground surrounding the church, among them the famous General Anthony Wayne, a hero of the American Revolution.

We go out into the burial ground, with the old stone grave markers carved with sentiments such as "At Rest" and "Asleep in Jesus," and Agnes takes me to see a particular row of gravestones that mean a great deal to her. They are not the gravestones of General Anthony Wayne or any of the other historical figures, but the gravestones of four small children, all from the same family, all of whom died in childhood.

"Just imagine," Agnes says, "all of them, four children, and from one family. Just think of the tragedy—the *immensity* of the tragedy. You know, they talk about soap opera. You couldn't *have* four children from the same family die on a soap opera. They'd say it was too much, it was a melodrama, an exaggeration. But there they are. It happened."

As we walk back to the car, slowly, Agnes says despite the tragedy borne in these stones she is not simply depressed by it, she is also inspired and encouraged by imagining the lives of those people:

"You think of the sorrow, yes, but the joy there must have been, too. Thoreau talked about 'lives of quiet desperation,' and of course there have been those lives, and there are such lives, but there also have been and are lives of quiet *valor*. And when you think that these people, the people buried here from two centuries ago, they had so little in material things, but they just kept going. There seems to be so little of that now. So many people now say they're looking for 'peace,' but peace has to be worked for, it has to be earned—you can't buy it, like hair spray, or an atomizer of cologne."

Driving back to Agnes' house, I tell her I was moved by "her church" and the cemetery, that in fact it's the only time I've been emotionally moved by a cemetery since I visited the famous "Sleepy Hollow Cemetery" in Concord, Massachusetts, where so many of the great nineteenth-century writers are buried. There is Emerson in stately grandeur, and

Thoreau with a plain little marker that says only "Henry," and all the Alcotts, including Bronson and Louisa May, in a family plot enclosed by grand, heavy chains. I say how impressive it is to see such history, literary history, all in that ground.

"Well, I know that must be interesting," Agnes says. "I'm sure it is. But what moves me about the graves of those children is they were just ordinary people, their family were just ordinary people. And they had to take all that, they had to bear it, and keep going on."

Yes, I say, I see what she means. And I do. It is part of the fact, a central part, of why she is a storyteller of and for "ordinary" people. Because that is what moves her, that is what interests her, and those things can't be faked.

Back at her house, the rambling white house with the black shutters, surrounded by giant pines, we walk a little before going in and she says the pine trees mean a lot to her, too, thinking how old they are.

"I really have an affinity for things that are old," she says. "I guess you could say I'm hooked on the past."

Says Agnes, smiling, looking up at one of those looming, ancient trees. The very act of following it with your eyes to the top can make you dizzy. I blink, and look down again.

"Well, why don't we go in and have a cup of coffee," Agnes says.

I follow, smiling, appreciating the practical suggestion of coffee after the awesome heights of hoary trees and the depths of tragically early graves. I have glimpsed a little of Agnes' world, and, as I follow her into the kitchen, I know where I am. I don't mean geographically, but in spirit and instinct.

This, in the end, is where Agnes has brought us, we who are a part of the audience and so are all her children; this is her gift, to bring us here and make us believe it, make us feel we belong and share in it, even if only through her imagination and then our own.

Home.